HUMANITARl

RONY BRAUMAN

Humanitarian Wars?

Lies and Brainwashing

In conversation with
Régis Meyran

HURST & COMPANY, LONDON

Originally published as Guerres humanitaires, mensonges et intox
© Éditions Textuel, 2018
13 Quai de Conti – 75006 Paris
www.editionstextuel.com

First published in the United Kingdom in 2019 by
C. Hurst & Co. (Publishers) Ltd.,
41 Great Russell Street, London, WC1B 3PL
© Rony Brauman, 2019
Translator Nina Friedman
All rights reserved.
Printed in India

Distributed in the United States, Canada and Latin America by
Oxford University Press, 198 Madison Avenue, New York, NY 10016,
United States of America.

A Cataloguing-in-Publication data record for this book
is available from the British Library.

This book is printed using paper from registered sustainable
and managed sources.

ISBN: 9781787382169

This book is printed using paper from registered sustainable
and managed sources.

www.hurstpublishers.com

I would like to thank Marc Le Pape for his careful review and invaluable comments.

CONTENTS

Foreword (Régis Meyran)   ix

1. What do we mean by "just wars"?   1

The criteria that have defined "just war" since
Thomas Aquinas are intended to limit both
the reasons for going to war and the methods
employed. The UN recycled them in 2005
under the "Responsibility to Protect" doctrine.

**2. Using "alternative facts" to justify war:
the case of Libya**   23

The propaganda leading up to the 2003 Iraq
invasion, which centred on "weapons of mass
destruction", did not convince people outside
the United States. In contrast, the equally false
allegations against the Gaddafi regime had
majority support in France, including among
those who mocked America's gullibility.

3. Somalia: the first humanitarian war   47

Somalia was the laboratory where the UN
tested its first militarized rescue operation. A
famine was wreaking havoc in the midst of

civil war and drought, but armed force was not the only possible response.

4. Kosovo: a morally justified unjust war?   65
Europe had legitimate reasons for opposing a violent ethnic-based power on its soil, but the diplomatic conference convened for that purpose appears to have been just window dressing for the American push for war.

5. Afghanistan and Iraq: two wars "for civilization"   77
While an army is the right tool for fighting another army, it is not the appropriate way to start a democratization movement. Yet that is what we continue to expect, using women's bodies as an indicator of progress.

6. International humanitarian law: legal pipe dream and the language of power   89
Since the late nineteenth century, pacifists have viewed humanitarian law as a means for making war acceptable, and thus more likely. The recent development of killer robots and other "smart weapons", presented as "humanitarian progress", demonstrates the prescience of their critique.

Notes   111

FOREWORD

Many observers believe we have entered a "post-truth" era, in which the very notion of truth has been discredited. News from the mainstream media is questioned on social media, conspiracy theories spread like wildfire, and populist leaders feel free to spout—as a Trump administration spokesperson did recently—"alternative facts" to dispute journalists' observations. Some might argue that the powers that be have been distorting the facts for a while now, especially in propaganda from fascist and authoritarian regimes (take, for example, the infamous photograph of Stalin with his friends who were "edited out", one by one, as they fell victim to the Great Purge). And that is true. But we tend to think that under democratic regimes—except in the particular case of "populist" ones—we are naturally protected from falsified facts. Yet when it comes to war, this does not seem to hold. That is what Rony Brauman—well-known physician, humanitarian, and former president of Médecins Sans Frontières, a man who has been on the front line of many conflicts—is trying to tell us here, and the unorthodox conclusions he draws from them may well raise some hackles. Talking about Somalia, Kosovo,

Afghanistan, Iraq (phase 2) and Libya, he gets straight to the point: what characterizes those wars is "the power of propaganda, once it takes root in favourable intellectual soil". Because for him, each of those conflicts, rationalized by "humanitarian" imperatives, was based on lies, and was in reality a moral crusade portrayed as a grand battle between good and evil. Once the war was won, it was assumed, democracy would naturally blossom under the benevolent supervision of the West.

Yet none of that is real. Wars can be triggered by irrational fear and to distract the public's attention; often they are never really "won", but go on to produce countless complications. In these pages Brauman explains the ways in which "democracies and dictatorships are not, in fact, all that different" in war situations. Though he is not an absolute pacifist, he argues that Western leaders should adhere as closely as possible to the idea of "just wars" to avoid fighting wars for dubious moral reasons, in particular "humanitarian" pretexts.

We hope that this dialogue—which treads a fine line between much-needed criticism of government propaganda and a refusal to descend into conspiracy theory—helps readers sharpen their critical thinking.

Régis Meyran

WHAT DO WE MEAN BY "JUST WARS"?

In this conversation we are going to try to explain why you are criticizing a series of wars conducted by the West (often with French support), which the media and politicians portrayed as "just" or even "humanitarian". To begin, which are these so-called "just" wars, and what do they have in common?

By "just wars" I mean wars ostensibly motivated primarily by humanitarian concerns, that is, the protection of civilian populations: saving a population from famine (Somalia 1992), impending massacre (Kosovo 1999 and Libya 2011), and oppression (Afghanistan after 2002). And as a backdrop I'll include wars that political forces called for, but didn't conduct, in the name of those same principles—like Rwanda during the genocide and Darfur during the "Save Darfur" campaign. Our conversation will be about all of these.

I draw a distinction between these and other wars or military operations fought in the name of security, such as the wars in Afghanistan (2001–2), Iraq (2013–) and Mali (2013–), or in support of a government or United Nations force (Sierra Leone (2000) and Côte d'Ivoire (2002–11), as well as shorter or limited interventions that were not wars, strictly speaking, such as Operation Artemis in the Democratic Republic of Congo (2002) and Operation Sangaris in the Central African Republic (2013–16), also fought in support of armed UN interventions.

So what distinguishes these so-called "just wars" is the "humanitarian" motives for intervention, which the other wars don't have. But haven't all of the wars conducted by the West been presented as "just" at some point?

Indeed, the humanitarian motive is mainly what distinguishes "just wars" from the others; it is also the reason why "just wars" and "humanitarian wars" are now synonymous. But the distinction between these and other wars needs to be clarified. First, the distinction does not imply, a priori, any value judgment on my part, since I may have approved of or, on the contrary, criticized wars in each of the above-mentioned groups. For example, I supported NATO's war in Kosovo but (as we will see) for different reasons from those given by NATO, while I criticized the wars in Somalia and Libya. Similarly, I consider several of the interventions or wars fought in the name of security justified, though I was critical of the craziest one, the Iraq invasion, as well as the second phase of the war in Afghanistan. But we'll get back to that later.

Some will no doubt object to the rather loose distinction between these two categories, in particular because, to those that supported them, all of the above-mentioned wars were virtuous undertakings aimed at a greater good—a necessary evil. True. No one—not even Hitler or Pol Pot or Assad—wants evil for evil's sake. I consider the distinction relevant, however, even essential, to a specific subject—so-called "just" or "humanitarian" wars—for three reasons: (1) humanitarian rhetoric dominated the justification for war; (2) that rhetoric was based on false claims; and (3) the themes of that rhetoric form the core of the "Responsibility to Protect" doctrine adopted by the UN's 2005 World Summit, which re-established the legality of the older, "just war" concept.

Why is the idea of "just war", in itself, a problem?

First, because while claiming to protect populations, the UN is rehabilitating war, when in fact it was created to prevent it. In addition, the total number of deaths—tens of millions—caused by the five permanent members of the Security Council since 1945 certainly justifies any reluctance to entrust them with protecting human rights in the world through military intervention. Especially since the UN, in granting itself the right to declare war and to call it "just", is acting as both referee and player, and legalizing the confusion between judges and parties to a conflict. At the time that declaration was made, I found those arguments sufficient to reject the very notion of "just war" as a contradiction in terms; war is a lie, war is hell, it can never be "just". But unless I wanted to take a radical pacifist position—which I respect but do not share—I felt it necessary to understand the exceptions, that is, the situations in which war might be justified, and on what terms.

So to continue that line of reasoning ... "Just" or "humanitarian" war is therefore based, legally, on the "responsibility to protect"; can you explain what that phrase means?

The "responsibility to protect" or, in international jargon, "R2P" comes from the title of a report written by a commission of "high-level people"—officially known as the International Commission on Intervention and State Sovereignty (ICISS)—that the Canadian government put together in December 2000 in response to a question from UN Secretary-General Kofi Annan regarding the criteria governing "humanitarian interventions". I should point out that in English "humanitarian intervention" refers to armed interventions, which is not necessarily the case in French. Canadian general Roméo Dallaire, who commanded the UN force in Rwanda (UNAMIR) during the genocide, played a major role in popularizing that idea. Basically, the legitimacy of the use of force rests on the seriousness of the threat (mass atrocities), on its being used only as a last resort, and on the proportionality of the response. It is up to the Security Council to determine whether the following criteria are met: just cause, last resort, proportionality, and legitimate authority. There one would find, together with "reasonable chance of success", the classic criteria for "just war" that have been around since Thomas Aquinas.

But what makes this report important? Did UN leaders use it to justify their shift from a culture of peacekeeping to a culture of war?

Let's just say that the report officially broadened the criteria for engaging in war (*jus ad bellum*) without creating any new mechanisms. Chapter VII of the UN Charter states that the Security Council may decide to use force if it finds "the existence of any threat to the peace, breach of the peace, or act of aggression". It has done so on several occasions, most notably in Korea (1950), the Congo (1961) and Iraq (1991). From this perspective, the R2P is limited to confirming that mass atrocities might constitute a threat to peace. There have been innumerable seminars, colloquia, articles and books devoted to the subject since 2005, most in support of what was seen as a fresh impetus, a moral awakening in the world of heartless state interests. Such stirrings did not, however, grow out of a successful public relations effort only. They were a direct response to the justified sense of shame at the attitude of states during the Rwanda Tutsi genocide in 1994 and the contemporaneous war in Bosnia.

At the time, Kofi Annan was Assistant Secretary-General for Peacekeeping Operations—otherwise known as the head of the Peacekeepers. In particular, it was he who decided, under pressure from various member states, to pull nearly all of the Blue Helmets out of Rwanda on

20 April 1994, two weeks after the massacres began, reducing the force from 2,500 to 250. While keeping the 2,500 UNAMIR soldiers there wouldn't have changed anything militarily, at the time of the decision it could be seen only as a message of encouragement—albeit indirect—to the killers, and of abandonment to the victims. It was that abandonment in the face of what would turn out to be the "crime of all crimes", genocide, that the R2P was meant to address.

What could the peacekeepers, who are prohibited from using force, have done?

In thinking about this, we have to keep in mind that neither the civilian nor military components of the Rwandan government were fully on board with the genocide plan. It wasn't until the Hutu extremists took power in mid-April that government resources were used to wipe out the "domestic enemy", although extremist militias had been ready to get to work long before then. The researcher André Guichaoua[1] showed that prior to 6 April, the government was mixed, and that the genocide began with the coup—something also confirmed by the International Criminal Tribunal in Arusha.

Keeping the 2,500 UNAMIR peacekeepers in Rwanda might have helped support the law-abiding elements within the government army, giving them the ability to neutralize the genocidal pro-coup leaders and their troops. That political option was not tried. The massacre, on 7 April, of ten Belgian peacekeepers escorting the prime minister undoubtedly played a role, likely resonating, in the minds of the Security Council, with the very recent and disastrous outcome of the UN's intervention in Somalia, from which the last American troops had withdrawn just two weeks earlier. Boutros Boutros-Ghali claimed that 5,000 well-trained men, if mobilized in time, could have halted the Tutsi genocide. I would agree, provided such intervention had taken place within two weeks of the attack on the president's plane, while high-level Rwandan army officers opposed to the massacres were still in place and in favour of out-side military help against the putschists. But what was possible during that brief period later became impossi-ble, because the putschists had taken power.

After the coup, the political reality in Rwanda was that of a war between the Rwandan Patriotic Front (RPF) and the "interim government" (i.e. the genocidal putschists), each wanting to hold on to its power or take all the power for itself. In that context, intervening would not have meant taking a position between the two, but either fighting and defeating them in order to set up a UN trusteeship over the country—which would have been legally possible but politically impracticable—or siding with the RPF rebellion to overthrow the interim government. The latter was politically inconceivable given the circumstances in Rwanda, if for no other rea-son than that the RPF fully intended to take power with-out having to answer to any authority whatsoever.

In addition, the massacres occurred barely a month after the last GIs had left Somalia under a cloud of fail-ure and of humiliation of the international forces by armed Somali groups. That made getting involved in a local war—at the risk of becoming one of the factions, as happened in Somalia—unthinkable at the time. Could the "Elite Force"-type plan envisioned by Boutros-Ghali have been implemented in such a short time frame, something that would have been necessary for success? That's for each person to decide for himself. Personally, I have my doubts, owing to the practical and political complexity of armed international interventions, which were incompatible with the extreme urgency of the Rwandan situation.

Nevertheless, many human rights and humanitarian NGOs welcomed the R2P ten years later as a step forward, a sign of revival of their much-loved multilateralism and a collective commitment to no longer tolerate mass atrocities.

Let's talk a bit more about this report, "The Responsibility to Protect"; what do you think of the intervention criteria, as defined by the UN?

As I said, there are four criteria: (1) the decision to intervene must be made by the United Nations Security Council, i.e. the legitimate authority; (2) the violence of the response must not exceed that of the atrocities, i.e. the principle of proportionality; (3) all other means—diplomatic and economic means such as public condemnation and financial sanctions, in particular—must have been tried, i.e. the principle of last resort; and (4) there must be a reasonable chance of success.

The first two criteria—"legitimate authority" and "proportionality of the response"—are legal in nature, falling under international law. I won't spend a lot of time on this, except to point out that legal decisions are not necessary just, and vice versa. For example, while the Kosovo war wasn't "legal", because it was decided outside the Security Council, one can argue that it was legitimate; and while the war in Libya was legal, its legitimacy is debatable. Proportionality means using "sufficient"—that is to say, not excessive—violence. Never mind that every one of the Security Council's permanent members is a nuclear power and that nuclear deterrence relies precisely on the disproportionate damage suffered in the case of a nuclear attack.

The last two criteria are far more interesting to me, because they are more political, or politico-ethical. How long can one negotiate, use diplomacy and gesticulate in order to play for time? How much violence can one tolerate while hoping to stop it by non-violent means? The question of last resort and of reasonable chance of success implies an ability to calculate the final outcome. As Michael Walzer reminds us, "The object in war is a better state of peace"[2]—that is, a more secure situation than what existed before. And there lies the crux of the problem: how do we define success? At what point does the chief of staff come and tell the UN Secretary-General, "Mission accomplished"? We all remember the infamous "Mission accomplished" of George W. Bush, dressed up as a pilot and posing on an aircraft carrier, after the fall of Baghdad. And we know what happened after that.

In a public debate on the "right to intervene", in the midst of Libyan war, political scientist Pierre Hassner[3] cited these two contradictory ideas from Clausewitz: on one hand, no sensible person would start a war without a clear idea of what they hope to accomplish with the war and how they want to conduct it. On the other hand, because of friction, the fog of war, and changing means leading to changing objectives, no war ends as originally planned.

These two ideas, synthesized by Hassner, sum up the inherent practical contradiction whenever one goes to war, whether humanitarian or not: while a clear idea of the ends and the means is essential, the unforeseeable dynamics of the war make that impossible. He infers from this that it is impossible to formulate a general law of armed intervention, but argues that the question needs to be asked in particular situations. I agree with this measured approach, provided it's applied with the necessary rigour. To illustrate his position, Hassner cited Boutros-Ghali's statement about the 5,000 men who could have stopped the Tutsi genocide, an assertion that, as I told you, I found unrealistic.

Just to make sure I understand you correctly: even though recent wars were started on false pretences and claimed to be "humanitarian", you nevertheless find the last two UN criteria establishing the conditions for "just war"— that is, "war as a last resort" and "reasonable chances of success"—useful? Why? Is that a good synopsis of what a truly "just" war should be?

Yes, I think that basically sums it up. And I have to give the authors of "The Responsibility to Protect" credit for making reference to those concepts. In practice, however, the obligation to ensure that war was indeed the last resort was deliberately ignored in the conflicts we'll be looking at. As for "reasonable chances of success", these are impossible to assess when the stated aims are vague and general—like democracy, women's liberation, general well-being, and so forth. Or as Michael Walzer more bluntly puts it, "but foreign intervention, if it is a brief affair, cannot shift the domestic balance of power in any decisive way toward the forces of freedom, while if it is prolonged..., it will itself pose the greatest possible threat to the success of those forces."[4] They can, however, be assessed when the aims are precise and narrow—like forcing an occupying army to withdraw (Kuwait 1991 and Timor 1999), taking control of a limited area (Kosovo 1999), defending an existing government against a militia (Sierra Leone 2000), or destroying terrorist training camps (Afghanistan 2001). Although there aren't many examples, they do exist, showing that this criterion deserves to be taken seriously. A truly "just" war, ultimately, is a war (1) that one actively tried to avoid; (2) whose cause is prima facie justifiable; and (3) whose objective is well defined and achievable.

Do you mean that those last three criteria for "just war" are admirable in theory, but are not used as they should be and not thought out well enough in practice?

What I mean is that in many situations other than the ones I just cited, those criteria are only used as justification after the fact. The decision was made for certain undisclosed reasons and justified by different reasons, such as allowing Afghan women to remove their veils, WMD [weapons of mass destruction] in Iraq, or preventing a predicted slaughter in Libya.

With regard to the legal apparatus of the "responsibility to protect", you mentioned criteria that you think are intelligent but aren't utilized, and are justified after the fact. Do you mean that a UN-led "just war" is impossible, that it's pure illusion?

No, that's not what I mean. I think there are interventions that are necessary, for example, wars of resistance against aggression, which everyone except absolute pacifists accepts. Outside that narrow context, however, things get complicated. But the fact that it's complex doesn't prevent us from delving into the question—on the contrary. For example, beyond what I was saying about justifiable wars, I think we can also differentiate between wars of choice and wars of necessity—or military engagements, more generally, since not all lead to war. I'm thinking of the French troops in Côte d'Ivoire and the Central African Republic (CAR); it would be misleading to say they were at war. It was really difficult for France, which already had a military presence in those countries, to stay out of the tragic events that were unfolding. Their objectives were limited in both nature and duration, and were, for the most part, achieved. The situation in Côte d'Ivoire is better now than it was during the operation. Unfortunately that's not the case in the CAR, where things are getting steadily worse, but the French forces were able to deter various attacks and bring some stability to part of the country. Not enough to justify Foreign Minister Le Drian's triumphant statement to the Parliament giving France credit for "inter-community reconciliation" and "rebuilding the Central African government" when the operation ended in October 2016. I'm not criticizing him for embellishing the results of Operation Sangaris, which was part of his job as minister, but for misrepresenting them by bolstering the illusion that the objectives were achievable. In the end, the operation did some good and didn't make the situation any worse. And that's not always the case—far from it.

And was it somewhat different with Mali? I'm not sure that intervention was really a success.

Nor am I. If truth be told, I don't have a strong position on that conflict, nor do I have a clear idea about what more should be done in Syria. I wonder whether Dominique de Villepin was right in criticizing the French Army's overly-ambitious goals in Mali and the region, arguing that stopping the jihadists' advance toward Bamako was both necessary and sufficient. That case illustrates the tension so aptly summed up by Clausewitz; the stated objective was based on a changing reality, and its initial clarity—however clever—disappeared. I should note that it's especially hard to know what happened, since the information is locked away and Parliament has been kept in the dark about those operations—a serious anomaly in a democracy, which doesn't seem to bother many of our countrymen. Except for former Defence Minister Paul Quilès, hardly anyone seems interested and that's really unfortunate. That said, I think preventing Ansar Dine and AQIM (al-Qaeda in the Islamic Maghreb) from advancing toward Bamako was a legitimate goal.

In that particular case, the criteria for "just war" were met. AQIM posed a threat to the culture and democracy ...

Indeed, not to mention taking hostages, and so on. Stopping the jihadist advance toward the capital was a clear goal and had very realistic chances of success. The vast majority of Mali's people expected it. I would add that in politics, as in life in general, you can't wait until success is achieved. The question I feel unable to answer in this case—and in Syria—has to do with the limits of the intervention, not its existence.

You mentioned the historical roots of the "just war" concept ... What exactly are they?

The history of "just war"—or at least the glimpses I got from some readings on its Christian origins (though it exists in other traditions, as well)—convinced me that the concept is part of the lexicon of power. The first Christians, up to Augustine in the fifth century, forbade the use of swords and preached love of one's enemy. With the conversion of Emperor Constantine, Christians began to occupy positions of responsibility in the Empire. The pacifism of the early ages gave way to a reflection on the conditions that might justify war. "For it is the wrong-doing of the opposing party", wrote Augustine, "which compels the wise man to wage just

wars."[5] In the thirteenth century, Thomas Aquinas created a theoretical framework for it by setting out five
criteria that a war would need to meet in order to be
just; those criteria limited both the entry into war (*jus ad
bellum*) and the means employed in fighting it (*jus in bello*).
War was no longer self-evident, and the sovereign's
desire for it no longer sufficed.

**You go back to Thomas Aquinas's concept of
"just war", but is there a direct relationship
between the ideas of a thirteenth-century theo-
logian and those found today at the UN?**

There is a striking thematic continuity. Modern international humanitarian law (IHL) stems directly from *jus in
bello*, and the "responsibility to protect" from *jus ad bellum*. Whether they like it or not, humanitarians working
in war zones are tacitly accepting its logic, attempting to
alleviate the consequences and reduce "unnecessary cruelty", but not banish it. And that's what the principles
underlying the "just war" concept are aimed at. As a
humanitarian practitioner and member of an organization that has made war one of its fundamental fields of
action, I had to think about this. There was a tension
between rejecting the principle of war, an instinctive
humanitarian position, and accepting it in practice.
Especially since I was teaching courses (at Sciences Po[6]
and Manchester University) on the ethical and political
stakes of humanitarianism, and had to write about those
tensions, and, in explaining them, explain them to
myself. Or at least try to.

Your critique of "just war" and the "responsibility to protect" seems to suggest that one cannot decide, from the outside, that democracy is going to sprout naturally in a country by simply removing a given dictator. Is that why you've come out in favour of a kind of absolute non-interference? Take the case of Syria, for example.

I'm not for absolute non-interference, for the simple reason that it's not a tenable position. Western involvement has been necessary in Syria, due to the history and geography of the region and to the fact that the crisis is having a direct impact on Europe, and also to the legitimate expectations of some of the stakeholders, who are asking not for armed intervention but for political and military support. Moreover, involvement by some of the other states in the region, who have conflicting aims even when they are on the same side, is a reality that cannot be ignored, regrettable though it might be, and in turn requires that others get involved—in particular, permanent members of the UN Security Council. More generally, I feel that taking a non-interventionist position on principle is politically irresponsible.

An idea has emerged among the radical left, however, that we should not intervene because Western imperialism would be responsible for any consequences, or because armed assistance would necessarily be a disguised form of imperialism. What do you think about that?

Indeed. That's what we're seeing with the Syrian question, where there are convergences between the radical left, the nationalist right, and the extreme right, in the name of anti-imperialism for some and of anti-Islamism for others. And all share the mantle of ever-reliable secularism. The only morally coherent anti-interventionists are pacifists who reject the use of any type of violence, but that's obviously not the case with the people we're talking about here, who only reject violence when it comes from the opposing side.

French planes have also been criticized for dropping bombs on targeted areas, killing civilians. What is your opinion? Is it reasonable to think that there's another way to do things, or should we cynically acknowledge this as inevitable collateral damage?

However "surgical" they are, however carefully they are targeted, air strikes cause destruction beyond their theoretical objective. We cannot determine their effects with any mathematical certainty. Whenever you engage in armed conflict, there is always a risk of killing civilians—and people you don't want to kill, more generally, like friendly combatants—and it inevitably happens. It's just a question of degree.

That being said, I don't reject, out of hand, expressions some consider euphemistic or even anaesthetizing, such as "surgical strikes" and "collateral damage". Such terms can of course be used to mask terrible realities, but they can also reflect a real desire to take precautions in the conduct of war. For the people being bombed there's no difference, but precision weapons do spare some lives. So I draw a distinction between firing a missile at an identified military target and dropping explosives on a neighbourhood or the indiscriminate bombing of a city.

With regard to the Syrian conflict, which is very complex, can you remind us of the precipitating circumstances of the uprising?

During the first year of the uprising, a Syrian opposition emerged in the form of mass mobilization—large, peaceful, weekly demonstrations, which increasingly had to defend themselves as the government systematically attacked them with its snipers, militias and local paramilitary forces. For a year, the population and its leaders were able to resist such provocations, attempting to undermine the regime and break down its intransigence by means of mass demonstrations. The option of ousting the regime through violence was not, in fact, chosen until a year later, in the spring of 2012. That began a new phase of the rebellion, with the radicals taking control. When it comes to using violence, moderate and democratic opposition groups are at a disadvantage relative to radical groups, who believe that power grows out of the barrel of a gun, in both senses of the word. Power is gained by violence, and maintained that way as well. I should add that very early on, the regime released jailed Islamists—including some fearsome fighters and extremists—in order to poison the rebellion, taint its public image, and establish and reinforce its own pose as the protector of minorities and guarantor of public safety. The debate and controversy over this subject prove that Bashar al-Assad was successful, at least on this point.

This is illustrated, in particular, by statements from Carla Del Ponte, the former prosecutor for the International Criminal Tribunals for Rwanda and the former Yugoslavia, who dramatically resigned from the UN Commission of Inquiry on Syria, saying "everyone in Syria is on the bad side ... And the opposition is now made up of extremists and terrorists."

Six years after the initial uprising, Damascus appears to be on the verge of winning the war; the democratic revolt is losing its Western support, and terror attacks in Europe are strengthening the position of Assad, who is now backed by a de facto Russo-American coalition. The alliances within that coalition are complex and contradictory, with the United States strengthening its ties with Saudi Arabia against Iran and with the Syrian Kurds against their Turkish ally, while Russia feels free to bomb US-backed forces to support the Damascus–Tehran axis, as happened during the siege of Aleppo. A confusing situation if ever there was one, further complicated by the flow of fighters abandoning the democratic opposition to join the ranks of the jihadists, attracted more by the pay than by ideology, no doubt, but strengthening the latter at the former's expense.

The situation you describe is indeed hard to decipher, to the point that in an attempt to get a clearer picture some have tried comparing it to episodes from twentieth-century history. Jean-Pierre Filiu, for example, argued that the war in Syria is a bit like "our Spanish Civil War", an idea that was echoed somewhat in the press. Do you find that a valid comparison?

I have mixed feelings about that. Like many people, I think that we had a political and moral obligation to help the democratic opposition (we'll have to come back to what we mean by "democratic opposition" in these different conflict situations). But saying "it's our Spanish Civil War" is equivalent to saying that if we don't stop it, we are passively witnessing a trial run for the next world war. This *reductio ad Hitlerum* is more moral intimidation than a rational argument.

But the Spanish Civil War is not an absurd comparison, because there were factions on the Republican side that were anything but democratic. And the fact that they fought the fascists did not mean those components were themselves democratic. As we know, there was a civil war within the civil war in Spain, between the Stalinists on one side and the anarchist and Trotskyist Republicans on the other. And supporting the Republican side as a whole meant supporting the Stalinist camp.

The fact is that we don't know the exact nature or scope of Western support for the Free Syrian Army.[7] It exists, but is largely covered by military secrecy, so we can either deplore its absence, like Jean-Pierre Filiu or Bernard-Henri Lévy, or imply that it is significant, like the French government. We know for certain, however, that the opposition has been given sustained aid.

Be that as it may, the war in Syria is portrayed as "just" from the Western point of view. Is it really "just" or necessary, in your opinion?

I don't think it was portrayed that way. In any case, it isn't just or necessary, it's catastrophic. Once the political

uprising gave way to military insurrection, the democratic protest began to founder. It began fighting on
Assad's chosen turf—armed violence—and the country
was reduced to a heap of rubble whose recovery defies
imagination.

2

USING "ALTERNATIVE FACTS" TO JUSTIFY WAR

THE CASE OF LIBYA

Several recent wars have been portrayed as "just" in the West, yet you mean to show that they were based on a lie in the beginning. Please explain that.

What's striking when you look closely at the wars in Somalia, Kosovo, Afghanistan and Libya is the power of propaganda, once it takes root in favourable intellectual soil. That is to say, when it meets a horizon of expectation, when it is high enough on a social credibility scale. I make no distinction here between opinion that is informed and opinion that is not. "Alternative facts" have become a subject of general mockery thanks to statements by Trump's press secretary, but we forget that they reigned supreme during the 2011 Libyan Civil War.

Any difference between the hypothetical, the plausible and the factual disappeared.

Take the example of Libya. What, exactly, was the problem in that war?

Libya was France's Iraq War, except that it was "legal", having been authorized by UN Security Council Resolution 1973. Some legal experts questioned its broad interpretation by NATO, led by France, arguing in particular that offers to negotiate were rejected out of hand and that the rebels were given large quantities of weapons, contrary to the resolution's recommendation. The execution of Muammar Gaddafi, and the regime change that was obviously the aim of the intervention, were not part of the resolution either, of course. Other legal experts and observers felt that the spirit of the resolution was to protect the Libyan people, and that meant removing the mortal danger threatening them—that is, Gaddafi and his regime. That's what Sarkozy, Obama and Cameron said on 25 February, only a few days after the start of the Benghazi uprising and well before the resolution's passage on 17 March. So it came as no surprise when the "Guide" was killed and a new regime installed.

Can you remind us of the international context in which the Libyan Civil War took place?

This was February 2011, during the Arab anti-dictatorship uprisings. Sarkozy's government had been seriously damaged, in particular by odious statements from Michèle Alliot-Marie (then French Minister of Foreign

Affairs) offering to provide anti-riot gear to the Ben Ali regime in Tunisia, one of the region's harshest dictatorships. At this point I'd like to clarify that while Alliot-Marie's words shocked me, I did not agree with the people criticizing Sarkozy for his tepid support for the Arab Spring, or even for Gaddafi's infamous December 2007 visit. While it's true that our president at the time campaigned as a champion of international human rights, and women's rights in particular, those promises, as Chirac said, bound only those who believed them, and I was not among them. I don't believe that a state or group of states can hold itself up as a universal moral authority, still less when it's a former imperial power in regard to its ex-colonies. It's true that there were two human rights figures in the government at the time, Bernard Kouchner and Rama Yade,[1] which fuelled the belief in human rights diplomacy, that is, diplomacy based on dividing the world into democracies and dictatorships. But again, such pious utterances are aimed at believers. What state can draw that dividing line?

There are, however, dictatorships obvious enough to be labelled as such.

Yes, if you take Sweden and Syria as models, with one being the example of a democracy and the other a raging dictatorship. But most countries sit somewhere between these two extremes, neither black nor white, fluctuating between authoritarianism and liberalization. It's an abstraction—a kind of sanctimonious derealization, ridiculous at best and destructive at worst. The Sinologist Simon Leys, one of the few people to criticize

Maoism at its height,[2] described justice in the totalitarian world. The following, he wrote, are "the first three articles of such nonexistent institutions: (1) some cases should be treated with special benevolence; (2) other cases should be treated with special severity; and (3) this does not apply in all cases."[3] In my opinion, these three articles describe the reality of international relationships well.

Remember, for example, that in 2007 most of the presidential candidates who gathered in the great hall of the Mutualité conference centre—at Bernard-Henri Lévy's invitation, no doubt—promised to end the supposed genocide in Darfur, by force if necessary. I won't rehash the details of that campaign by American neoconservatives and their French counterparts;[4] suffice it to say that the point, again, was to go to war. There, too, they invented an enemy of humanity—a rapist-genocidal maniac—who had to be rendered powerless. And the same people were singing the praises of Paul Kagame, Africa's other mass murderer, who had just been "re-elected" with 98.79% of the vote (and 97% voter turnout) in Rwanda.

Let's get back to Libya. Are you condemning the somewhat facile position, which was common at the time, of those who were saying, "Look, Sarkozy invited Gaddafi, it's a scandal"?

Yes. Inviting Gaddafi to France seemed natural to me in return for the French head of state's earlier visit, during which lucrative contracts were signed by the same people who would later portray him as another Hitler—that is, Sarkozy and Kouchner. I should point out that the origin of that diplomatic exchange was the release of the Bulgarian nurses held hostage by the Libyan government and "freed" by Sarkozy, Gaddafi's gift to the new French president, in exchange for which he was promised a state visit and thus normalized relations. What I find shocking about the hostage release, in hindsight, was Sarkozy's astounding cynicism in interfering in the advanced stages of secret talks between the European Union and Libya, in order to reap the benefits. Be that as it may, it was only fair, and predictable, that Gaddafi would visit Sarkozy.

Alright, but where exactly was the lie?

On 21 February—that is, a few days after the first demonstrations in Benghazi—Al Jazeera reported that in Tripoli the Libyan Air Force was bombing protesters who had taken to the streets in solidarity with the victims of repression in Benghazi. That same day, Sarkozy, Obama and Cameron separately—but in remarkable concurrence—declared that Gaddafi had to go. What the three leaders said, in essence, was that a head of state who bombs his own people is not worthy of governing. Everything points to the fact that it was on that day that the plan for a punitive expedition came into being, since that's what was intimated by the thinly veiled words from the leaders of the three countries capable of launching military operations far from their bases. It was also the scene described by Bernard-Henri Lévy on the first page of his book on the Libyan Civil War, entitled "Scène de chasse à Tripoli" [Hunting scene in Tripoli]:[5] "It is always good to know when things started," he wrote, not without reason, right at the beginning, before detailing the images he saw on a TV screen at the Cairo airport, where he happened to be that 21 February: planes (Sukhois, he clarified, not Mirages) "diving on the crowd of unarmed demonstrators and strafing them". There follow myriad details, giving the sense of reality one expects from an eyewitness: a woman, dress lifted, spinning around, throwing herself face down, a group disappearing in a cloud of ash and smoke, a balcony in flames, a car rising off the ground, also in flames ... He sets the scene: "on one side the deadly weapons ..., on the other, the human anthill running in every direction." There's only one problem: that opening scene never happened; that "beginning" does not exist. I don't know which images Lévy was describing in such abundant detail, but there was no bombing in Tripoli, as the US Secretary of Defense and chairman of the Joint Chiefs of Staff acknowledged to Congress,[6] more truthful about that point than the French and British leaders. This episode is reminiscent of the famous vial of anthrax, satellite photos and portraits of al-Qaeda leaders that Colin Powell brandished in front of the Security Council on 5 February 2003 to prove, according to him, that there were weapons of mass destruction and Bin Laden henchmen in Baghdad. In the present case, however, it was mental images— images often talked about and described, but never seen. To quote Régis Debray, "We see much more with our ears than with our eyes" and he was never more right than with the Libyan question.

As if to force the issue even further, the Security Council unanimously decided on 26 February—only ten days after the uprising started—to refer the Libyan situation to the International Criminal Court (ICC), asserting that "the widespread and systematic attacks currently taking place … against the civilian population may amount to crimes against humanity" and emphasizing, in particular, "the need to respect the freedoms of peaceful assembly and of expression, including freedom of the media".[7] It listed the names of people who should be prosecuted, and the ICC rushed to start an investigation at the beginning of March. Such eagerness was unheard of at an institution known for extreme circumspection—and what's more, for a country that is a non-signatory to the Rome Statute. I would add that we know nothing about any "widespread and systematic attacks" in February, and that the ICC's sudden interest in freedom of expression appears to reflect the overzealousness of a criminal court ever submissive to the powerful.

So, according to you, the Libyan government didn't bomb its people. But if that event and those images don't exist, how did they come to be believed? And how can you say, with any certainty, that none of it existed?

The only sure thing about that event is that it didn't happen! Even so, and much to my regret, I'm unable to reconstruct how the brainwashing—which was the false basis for the war, the first in an interesting series—was accomplished. Not having access to the government archives, I have to settle for what's publicly available and what witnesses were able to tell me. Journalists who were in Tripoli at the time, whom I met with in March, assured me that there were no bombings in February, adding that in their opinion it was a psychological warfare operation by Qatar by means of that country's television station. Al Jazeera played a major role in the war, supporting the rebellion. It obviously didn't take that war to convince me of the importance of propaganda, but I'm still amazed, and sometimes saddened, by the passivity—even submissiveness—with which people allowed themselves to be brainwashed by the political and media consensus that was being created at that point in time. Because it didn't stop with the nonexistent bombing. A few days later, on 2 March, we learned during a press conference by the secretary general of the Libyan Human Rights League in Paris that 6,000 people had already been killed by the regime, 3,000 of them in Tripoli and 2,000 in Benghazi. This helped the White House's denial of the Tripoli attack—which, according to a press release posted on the White House website, was "no longer confirmed"—to pass unnoticed.

But what did that denial matter? Again, there was no a priori reason to question the statement—other than to distinguish the possible from the factual, which of course should be the basis of any news item. The regime and its leader were obviously capable of atrocities, although they could be blamed for "only" two mass killings from 1996, when they quelled the Derna uprising[8] and crushed the Islamist revolt at the Abu Salim prison. That was obviously more than enough to make the heavy death toll seem plausible, although, again, there were no images of killing fields or deadly attacks (as were seen elsewhere since smartphones had become common-place, in Syria in particular). The images distributed later as "evidence of massacres" actually showed the remains of Islamists killed at Abu Salim in 1996 and of camels. We later learned, however, from the original source of that "news" that the figures did not come from a count or assessment, but from a strategy to mobilize public opinion. We have to acknowledge it succeeded. Without much effort, it's true, so strong was the desire to believe it, but it succeeded. Subsequent investigations by Amnesty International and Human Rights Watch reported some 300 dead in the first month of the upris-ing, i.e. twenty times fewer, 100 of them in Benghazi. That included a significant percentage of combatants, because the uprising quickly turned into an armed insur-rection. I'm aware that when talking about human lives this numerical argument is distasteful, but calculating human losses is part of how we understand situations like this, though it is not the last word, and numbers were central to the various propaganda efforts in all of the conflicts we're discussing here.

Agreed, but wasn't the threat of a massacre hanging over the people of Benghazi?

Indeed, and that carnage—announced by Gaddafi's son—provided *ex post facto* justification for the interven-tion. Without ever acknowledging that they had been fooled by Al Jazeera and conveniently forgetting the fabricated strafing and fabricated killing fields they cir-culated, the vast majority of political commentators, of

31

all categories, still cite that announcement as fact. Notice that hardly anyone, aside from Lévy and the main protagonists, perhaps, still defends that armed intervention, given the subsequent disaster in the country and the region. On the other hand, none of those commentators consider it wise to wonder whether the threat was actually plausible.

Personally, I don't think it was, and I have good reasons for that. But before trying to expand upon that point, let's seriously consider the hypothesis. Had the line of tanks we heard so much about really been advancing on Benghazi, with its forward elements already in the immediate vicinity, it could have been stopped by a demonstration of force. Substantial military resources had already been deployed, and would have allowed that, especially since the pro-Gaddafi forces were exposed in the barren, rocky landscape, where they were spread out and easily visible, under close surveillance by American drones and satellites and thus extremely vulnerable.

It would thus have been possible to shield the city of Benghazi using clear warnings, overflights and shows of strength, even before creating a no-fly zone, which is an act of war. That was the spirit of Resolution 1973, which had been adopted on 17 March for that purpose. In addition, on 18 March, Gaddafi let it be known that he would agree to a ceasefire. That proposal was rejected immediately by rebel commander Khalifa Haftar and his new French, British and American allies. The proposal was reiterated on 20 March, with no further response. These may have been diversionary tactics on

Gaddafi's part, or he may have been playing for time. The fact is that he was militarily weak compared to the opposing forces, and politically weakened by the defection of many of his allies in Libya and abroad. The National Transitional Council (NTC), which Sarkozy recognized on 10 March as the "only legitimate representative of the Libyan people", was actually made up of dignitaries from the now-reviled regime. Attempting mediation under such conditions with a weakened government would in no way have been an act of appeasement, as supporters of the war liked to trumpet. The rebels were armed, and while they had suffered some serious setbacks in mid-March in several cities they had quickly seized control of, the regime had a gun to its head. The circumstances could have been conducive to serious negotiations on sharing and exercising power.

There were several other offers to mediate, in particular one on 27 March by Turkey, detailing its contacts on both sides, and by the African Union in early April, proposing a ceasefire followed by negotiations. As a precondition, the NTC demanded that Gaddafi step down, despite the fact that it was in theory an attempt to bring him to the negotiating table. Other offers for talks and cessation of hostilities came from Gaddafi in May and June, and all were disregarded for the same reason. I'm not surprised that Sarkozy and the Emir of Qatar ignored them, since I have no doubt that they wanted to get rid of Gaddafi, but I am still frightened by the calls of most editorial writers to carry on to the bitter end and the follow-the-herd mentality of the politicians (except for the French Communist Party)—in short, by the desire to do battle that I sensed growing, making them deaf to any possible deal.

So you believe, apart from the fact offers of mediation were deliberately ignored, despite everything, that it would have been possible to limit the military intervention to protecting the people of Benghazi if they were threatened. Yet you said you had doubts about that threat. Can you explain the contradiction?

Contrary to the impression I may have given thus far, I wasn't strongly opposed to the idea of intervention in the beginning, because I was not immediately aware of the ongoing brainwashing, starting with the infamous airstrike against the demonstrators in Tripoli. While it seems obvious to me that Sarkozy wanted war from the start, that's in hindsight, because he was very careful not to show it. He was still claiming to be open to compromise on 10 March. It wasn't until the UN resolution vote on 17 March—hastened by the supposed imminence of a Benghazi massacre—that the military option suddenly took centre stage, though the means had already been largely deployed. It began with an attack on four tanks that attempted to penetrate the city at dawn on 19 March, and we later learned that the Americans had fired a hundred or so Cruise missiles at Libyan military installations to enforce the no-fly zone. Robert Gates, then US Secretary of Defense, was apparently opposed to American involvement and had warned that creating a no-fly zone was an act of war. That's a useful detail, because we too often talk about no-fly zones as a way to

ensure peace through deterrence, forgetting that they sig-
nify opening fire by a foreign power in hostile territory.

**Alright, but when did you start doubting the
official explanations, and why?**

I started to form a clearer opinion on the issue while
listening to Patrick Haimzadeh—an ex-military Arabist
diplomat who knew Libya very well—analyze the political and military situation in Benghazi. He had a book
coming out at the time entitled *Au cœur de la Libye de
Kadhafi*,[9] and had been invited to appear, as a Libya spe-
cialist, on the popular TV talk show *Ce soir ou jamais*, on
which I was also a guest. It was 22 March, the day after
the French military success. I listened to Haimzadeh
reveal the disastrous scenario that continues to hold
sway today by showing that, in reality, the pro-Gaddafi
forces didn't have the means to carry out the threatened
bloodbath. With fewer than 1,000 men and about 20
tanks, they were in no position to take control of a city
of nearly a million people, extending over 300 square
kilometres, and historically opposed to Tripoli. Even
less so because the insurgents were armed and had
already repelled the tanks. Haimzadeh, who went on to
write a number of extremely interesting and well-docu-
mented articles on Libya,[10] had been a weapons inspec-
tor in Iraq in 2002. So he was no stranger to weapons
of mass destruction! I heard him make the comparison
between the "bloodbath prevented *in extremis*" and
America's infernal propaganda machine in 2003, but I
don't remember whether it was during that programme
or later.

Did the Libyan government really send tanks against the population?

The hundreds of tanks supposedly heading to Benghazi were never filmed, whether on the ground, from the air, or from space, while it would have been impossible to camouflage them in that landscape, spread out over such a distance. There are images of a line of pick-up trucks loaded with bags of food and fighters in mismatched uniforms that included two or three tanks, but nothing even remotely like the tanks being talked about. That said, there were indeed 30 or so tanks already posted at the gates of the city. Those were the ones destroyed by the French planes and also (especially) by the insurgents. According to local witness accounts, what people in Benghazi feared most were the planes. In hindsight, we know that that fear was unwarranted, but at the moment it justified creating the no-fly zone.

The 17 March vote authorizing the use of force based on the "responsibility to protect" was in no way a foregone conclusion. Russia and China abstained, and Europe was divided—in short, the victory must have seemed fragile to Sarkozy and his close allies. Hence the determination to create a de facto situation and declare war without delay. "It's five minutes to midnight," trumpeted Lévy; barbarism was going to win within minutes, enough of the dithering, urgent action was needed! It was that Fort Apache-type narrative, those "alternative facts"—as they say in the White House today—that Patrick Haimzadeh picked apart with military precision.

I paid special attention to what he was saying because I remembered things I had read about the crushing of Budapest in 1956, and I recalled that the forces that quelled the uprising were on an entirely different scale. I checked the next day: the USSR sent 2,500 tanks, 1,000 armoured vehicles, and 75,000 Soviet soldiers; a week later, the Red Army had regained control of the city, at a cost of about 4,000 dead and 20,000 wounded. As I recall, Haimzadeh was talking about 1,000 men and 30 tanks, and no one contradicted him; he also pointed out that the people of Benghazi were far better armed than those in Budapest.

That raises questions about the fabrication of information. Are the journalists who cover these types of events misinformed, or is the "just war" ideology so strong that it reshapes reality?

Journalists come in all types, including the very well-informed! I prefer to look at the question from a different angle, noting, on one hand, that French military interventions enjoy, on the whole and a priori, strong media support; and on the other, that Gaddafi's outrageous utterances and self-portrayal made him the perfect enemy. Putting those two things together, it's clear that we were witnessing a face-to-face confrontation between democracy and tyranny, between civilization and barbarism … in short, between Good and Evil. That sort of confrontation leaves little room for Cartesian scepticism or critical thinking, with the risk of looking at best like a useful idiot, and at worst like a real bastard. The same thing happened in 2005–8 during the war in Darfur. An accusation of genocide was as good as proof of genocide, even when it came from notorious liars like the American neocons. Anyone who questioned it and opposed military intervention was accused of siding with the "Islamofascists"—like in the good old days of Stalinism.

For good measure, I also remember the accusation about mass rape, launched on the strength of a photo of a Viagra bottle on a tank crew member's bag. The picture was published in April, after the war started, again by Al Jazeera. That bottle signalled the existence of a rape strategy, carried out by the regime's African mercenaries, providing further confirmation—as if it were needed—of Gaddafi's barbarity. Those mercenaries did exist, in the thousands, including seasoned fighters—Tuareg, in particular—and many others, who were signed up with no military experience and sent to the front as cannon fodder. There were also white mercenaries, South Africans, Serbs and others, but we didn't hear any rape accusations about them. As a result, all Blacks were suspected of being pro-Gaddafi rapists, and there were numerous indiscriminate attacks. Should that be counted as collateral damage from the propaganda?

Alright, let's accept that this Good vs Evil interpretation of events—which led to the fabrication of alternative facts—trumped everything. Then who started the war, and whose interests were in play?

Sarkozy deserves top billing. This war was his doing, but it was made possible by British and American involvement, and Qatar's as well, with the Arab League in tow. The Pentagon was reluctant, but Obama ruled in favour of Hillary Clinton, then Secretary of State and a well-known interventionist. So it was a neat diplomatic set-up instigated by the Élysée Palace, with Lévy as its tireless and effective mouthpiece.

I can only speculate, of course, on the interests in play and the circumstances that made the war possible. Gaddafi's political isolation was the key factor, in my opinion. Aside from the African Union, which has very little influence outside Africa, he had no significant support, but felt capable of defying—even provoking—his main interlocutors in both the Arab World and Europe. In the international arena you have to be either careful or well protected, and Gaddafi was neither. He made himself both vulnerable and detestable, especially in the eyes of Sarkozy. The amazing contracts he negotiated with France in 2008—which included sales of the Rafale aircraft, military equipment like helicopters, tanks and radar anti-aircraft systems, and EPR nuclear plants—turned out to be nothing more than smoke and mirrors. The political benefits from the Bulgarian hostage release had long passed; what was left was the cost of the Guide's controversial and widely criticized visit and the submissiveness with which his hosts acceded to his tantrums and whims. Once an inconvenient ally needing cajoling, Gaddafi had become a nuisance, although not all ties were broken. But politics is as much a matter of circumstance as of will, and along came the Arab Spring. The uprisings against those corrupt dictatorial regimes finally found support in Paris, if belatedly.

Among the regimes being challenged, Tripoli was the only one that was politically and militarily vulnerable, as Egypt, Syria, Bahrain and Tunisia were untouchable for different, but conclusive, reasons. As someone who had approved of the US invasion of Iraq and was clearly part of the neoconservative movement, it was Sarkozy's chance to make his own mark on history. Let me clarify, in passing, that I don't question his conviction that he was doing something good for the country, because—on the contrary—that's what I blame him for the most. Without the dream of being regarded by posterity as the benefactor of an oppressed people, I don't think he would have had the impetus needed. I do think, however, that there is a lot more to learn about this story— for example, about the suspicions that Gaddafi helped finance Sarkozy's 2007 campaign. A recent investigation by Fabrice Arfi and Karl Laske[11] reported that suitcases full of banknotes were passed to Claude Guéant via businessman Ziad Takieddine, the initial intermediary between Sarkozy and Gaddafi. The case is under investigation, so we will find out what happened.

So what we're seeing is a lie, perpetuated by several governments, which no one cared about?

Actually, in the six years since the war—and despite the alarming signals coming from Libya—France's National Assembly has not seen fit to investigate or inquire about it. In contrast, the British Parliament's Foreign Affairs Committee issued a report in September 2016. After an investigation and many hearings, it confirmed that the war had been "founded on erroneous assumptions", that the threat to Benghazi was "overstated", that there was no tangible evidence to base it on, and that France was pursuing its own specific interests such as helping the president out of a difficult political situation, expanding its influence in North Africa, and promoting the French Army and its equipment. This was upsetting to the newspapers and the politicians—even the Greens, in theory supporters of non-violence—who had been unstinting in their support. Understandably, the report got little coverage in France.

The Qataris played a key political role, neutralizing some of the criticism of the intervention as Western interference by "Arabizing" it with their active pres-ence—not just militarily, but in the media and diplo-matically, as well. The Arab League, more passive than enthusiastic, was no obstacle. The British and Americans insisted on using NATO; although that wasn't the origi-nal plan, it may have been a military necessity. One might wonder, however, how NATO went from being (at least in principle) a defensive and geographically circumscribed alliance to an offensive one (since the war in the former Yugoslavia, at any rate), whose area of intervention had in recent years grown well beyond Europe and the Atlantic to include Afghanistan and Libya, in particular.

So that was the political context. What can you say about Gaddafi's death?

That it was part of the war's strategy, as I told you from the outset. Let's review the facts: Gaddafi was captured by the insurgents on 20 October, after NATO planes bombed his convoy as it was leaving Syrte. He was lynched, and much of his entourage—several dozen people—was executed, as a Human Rights Watch investigation showed. There was a rumour that French Special Forces were involved in capturing and killing him, but to the best of my knowledge there has been nothing to back that up. It is not, however, unreasonable to think that the aim of an aerial attack on an unarmed convoy was to kill the passengers, and in fact Gaddafi's vehicle was hit, and he was wounded, as a video shot by the rebels showed. I won't, for lack of evidence, go out on a limb and say that his death was engineered by France, but I have some serious suspicions about that. Because with victory approaching, the question "what to do about Gaddafi?" was becoming a pressing one. It must have been discussed at the highest levels. Capturing Gaddafi would have meant a trial in The Hague before the ICC, where the revelation of secrets both large and small, inconvenient for French government, would have been likely. Was his elimination planned? Was it a question of neutralizing a dangerous blackmailer, or was it a mishap, a kind of collateral damage?

Turning to the aftermath of the war, some also suggest that what was missing was an international commitment to post-conflict reconstruction. What are your thoughts about that?

Indeed. While everyone, or nearly everyone, now agrees that it was a disaster, most of the people who approved of the intervention credited it with preventing a bloodbath in Benghazi, as we discussed, and regret that it wasn't followed by a peacekeeping operation. Despite all the evidence, they assume that deploying peacekeepers to support the "state-building" (as they say in international newspeak) process would have helped stop Libya from descending into civil war.

That assumption doesn't hold for two reasons: first, because no peacekeeping mission has yet miraculously managed to keep a nonexistent peace, and it's hard to see why Libya would have been the first. And, second, a peacekeeping mission was explicitly precluded from the beginning, because the rule was: no foreign troops on Libyan soil. But even if that rule had been revised because of the circumstances, we would have been back to the previous problem—that is, the inability of peace-keepers to impose peace and establish the rule of law. Who really believes that the militias would have willingly turned over their weapons to foreign forces and taken their recommendations? This is a constant in the dominant discourse in this area—that is, a priori faith in the virtues of strength, even when it is essentially symbolic in nature, as is the case with UN peacekeepers. That irrational belief, unsupported by any empirical evidence, seems to stem from a refusal to imagine the limitations of what can be achieved by force, and from an illusion of omnipotence in which we (Westerners) are capable of solving such problems if only we have the will to do so. While history cannot serve as a guide or moral code, it can help us reflect. For example, we should ask ourselves why—with the exception of post-World War II Germany and Japan—no democracy has ever been established by a foreign army. Unless we can explain that fact, we must take it into account.

Libya subsequently sank into instability and unrest ... but there's nothing to indicate that things would have taken a peaceful course without intervention, agreed?

That's true. I'm not claiming that the more-or-less nascent civil war, fragmentation and violence that we've seen since 2011 wouldn't have occurred if France and her allies hadn't intervened. That no one can provide a counterfactual account—that is, describe, in a credible way, what would have happened had that been the case—in no way diminishes my critique, for one essential reason: the obvious, insurmountable inability to control the effects of the process which the intervention set in motion. I'm not talking about "collateral damage", which was very limited, thanks to the precautions that were taken. The bombing of Syrte—Gaddafi's home town, where he took refuge in July or August 2011—was an exception to the rule of caution that was in effect followed, and I don't think we can blame NATO forces for the thousands of deaths claimed by some opponents of the war. If you look at the destruction caused by American troops in Afghanistan, Pakistan and Iraq, or, much worse, by Russian forces in Syria, the difference in how the war was conducted is unmistakable.

And the argument that the Syrian situation proves that non-intervention is worse than intervention doesn't stand up to scrutiny. Syria's domestic and regional situation is very different from Libya's, and the blame for how bad things have got in that country lies with too much foreign intervention, not too little. In contrast to what is happening in Syria, no allied governments were willing to fight alongside the Gaddafi regime, which had to rely on mercenaries to reinforce its troops. Not only did Gaddafi have no credible international support; he was shaky domestically, as the very rapid defections among his entourage showed. That is the exact opposite of what is happening in Syria.

Wouldn't negotiation have been a more appropriate solution?

It isn't certain, as I said before, that Gaddafi would have agreed to really negotiate with the insurgents to find a political way out of the crisis. What is certain, however, is that the political route wasn't even given a chance, and that reasons were invented to torpedo the existing proposals and go straight to war. As Colin Powell famously said about Iraq: "You break it, you own it."[12] I think that remark does a good job of summing up the problem, which I'll restate as follows: we (the outside participants) did not have the means to control the consequences of our decisions. Beyond the lies that we talked about, this is the fundamental point, in my opinion, and it was obvious from the outset. That's why I called the decision to go to war irresponsible. As Clausewitz's bleak comments about the unpredictable nature of war—evoked by Hassner, and mentioned earlier—remind us, war, once launched, does not follow a ballistic trajectory—that is, a calculable plan. Quite the contrary. It is like lighting fuses for which you can't predict either the path or the resulting explosions: fragmentation, new actors (like jihadists), the spread of arms caches, unintended damage, and so forth.

So Libya was not a "just war" ... Was getting involved in the conflict even consistent with the responsibility to protect?

Going back to our criteria for "just war", we see that while the legal criteria (legitimate authority and proportionality) were met, the political criteria (last resort and reasonable chances of success) were ignored, though it is the latter that determine, in large part, the practical consequences. Had the intervention been limited to protecting Benghazi, leaving it to Libyan political stakeholders to negotiate on a level playing field, that criticism would be meaningless. But the opposite happened. It was a different case in the former Yugoslavia, both in Bosnia and in Kosovo, because Europe was able to act as a de facto authority in the aftermath of the intervention and limit potential excesses and unintended consequences. Haimzadeh was right to draw a parallel between how the wars in Libya and Iraq started. In France we mocked the gullibility of the Americans and their press, much of which—and especially the most prestigious publications—actively parroted all of the White House's lies. Yet with the exception of some in the media, there was the same headlong rush to war in France in 2011.

3

SOMALIA

THE FIRST HUMANITARIAN WAR

You're telling us that for the past few years, many of the wars led by the West have been portrayed as "just" and necessary for humanitarian reasons. In your opinion, what was the first "humanitarian war"?

Somalia was the scene, in the early 1990s, of the first "humanitarian war" of the post-Cold War era. In fact, the term first made its appearance in the press, at least in France, in reference to that international military intervention in Somalia, then in the grip of war and famine. It had all the elements: gangs of hoodlums looting aid shipments, clan militias taking food from children's mouths, calls for military intervention to put a halt to those barbarous acts …

Let's look more closely at the war in Somalia. And let's start with the facts: those violent clan

militias actually existed, and the famine as well, right?

Of course. Just as Gaddafi's dictatorship wasn't mere propaganda, the famine was real, as were the civil war and the inter-militia fighting. What I want to talk about is the narrative created from it, and the way the number of victims was manipulated to justify armed intervention.

Meaning what? Please explain how it is possible to go from proven facts to Western propaganda.

Again, let's look at the local and international context at the time. Somalia, under dictator Mohamed Siad Barre, descended into civil war in the late 1980s. Its territorial claims to majority-Somali regions in its neighbours, Kenya and Ethiopia (which it had attacked in 1977 in an unsuccessful attempt to take Ogaden), were nothing new. Ethiopia was supporting the Somali National Movement (SNM), an opposition group in the north of the country, with training and arms. Siad Barre, who had himself come to power by a coup d'état (in 1969), was deposed on 29 January 1991. The war, which had already killed tens of thousands in the north, then spread across the country.

The dictator's fall was barely noticed, having been overshadowed in the news by the start of the US offensive in the Gulf on 17 January. Mogadishu, the country's capital and main port, was split between the SNM's two rival leaders, Ali Mahdi and Mohamed Aidid. Brutal clashes alternated with periods of calm, with the country divided according to clan affiliation.

The existence of clans—just like lineages in other African countries with traditional and pre-state societies—is important to understanding the logic of war (which has been well studied by political anthropology) …

Detailing those affiliations would take us too far afield of our subject, and I wouldn't be able to describe them in any case. I'll confine myself to just a few comments: clans are solidarity groups claiming a common male ancestor, with the various clans claiming a common origin as well. That clan-based view of the Somali nation went hand in hand with a fairly non-hierarchical social organization, allowing its leaders to present their country as the only true African nation-state, where only a single language was spoken and only a single religion practised, or nearly so. So we see that, if need be, the illusion of a common origin and culture is no guarantee against divisions. When there is no government, solidarity groups emerge as the only source of security, in terms of either food and survival or protection, but that doesn't mean everyone is fighting everyone else. Talks, trade, alliances and counter-alliances create space for negotiation—volatile, it's true, but very real. Somalia is divided along other lines, as well: between the north, which is mainly pastoral, and the south, which is more sedentary; and between what was British Somaliland (which declared independence in 1991) and what was Italian Somalia, just to name the most obvious. What I mean is that Somalia has a society with its own way of doing things, its own divisions and its own rules. Mundane though it may be, that observation is necessary given the simplistic representations of homogeneous clans and ruthless militias spreading terror and destined to conduct merciless war. The epitome of this was the Ridley Scott film *Black Hawk Down*, which portrayed the disastrous punitive expedition in October 1993 by American Special Forces against Mohamed Farah Aidid, which ended in bloodshed, with 19 Rangers and hundreds of Somalis killed.

What part of the population was actually affected by the famine?

The famine first hit the people displaced by the war, not the general population. Though the administration had obviously collapsed, it had never been strong—it was at most violently repressive. Somalia is an arid country, and there was a drought, so stocks were meagre and life was precarious. Because the several thousand combatants engaged in fighting each other didn't want to, and couldn't, plunder the entire country, life went on, through the highs and lows, despite the instability and violence. But as the months wore on, more and more villagers fled the intense local fighting, and it was among that extremely vulnerable population, displaced by war, that the famine grew. As their numbers swelled and resources dried up, it was those several hundred thousand people who slipped from vulnerability to food shortages, and then to famine, in 1992. An MSF nutritional survey in the spring of 1992 reflected that reality; in the beginning, the host villages—chosen, of course, based on affiliations and alliances—helped the displaced.

But that couldn't last, given the insecurity I spoke about. The MSF survey showed that one out of every four children in that population had died in the previous six months, and that the majority of the survivors had severe malnutrition. That was not the case with the resident population, only marginally affected by the war. Those quantitative data substantiated what had as yet been only a rumour of famine. And this was the practical reason for doing and releasing the survey: a massive increase in emergency food aid was needed—it was imperative and it was feasible. And today I would add that it was imperative *because* it was feasible. In order to make an impact on public perception, MSF announced that if nothing were done for the displaced population, every child under five would be dead within a year. I'm not sure that extending the mortality curves that way was very rigorous, but we wanted to mobilize people and make an impact. Much to my chagrin, those figures were among those used by Boutros-Ghali to justify armed intervention. But I'm getting ahead of myself …

Why wasn't that vitally important food aid sent? It sounds as though all it would have taken was a decision to do it.

There was aid, but not enough, and the World Food Programme (WFP)—the UN agency responsible for these types of operations—felt that it couldn't do more for security reasons. Admittedly, at that point the WFP had been operating in stable environments and had no experience with that type of situation. Since then it has gained such experience, and would probably respond differently today. But had someone really wanted to go there, other organizations—NGOs, the International Federation of Red Cross and Red Crescent Societies— could have been mobilized and potentially stemmed the famine. And while the insecurity was real, with convoys being attacked and some of the aid diverted, a few organizations were ready to go and more joined them in the spring and summer of 1992, showing that the work was possible in practice. The International Committee of the Red Cross (ICRC), together with the Somali Red Crescent Society and some women's organizations, did remarkable work in the form of a large-scale food supply distribution network that served some two million people, even in the hardest-hit regions.

But the initial response of the powers concerned—the Security Council, UN agencies and donor governments— was expressed in law-and-order terms, that is, by the decision to send UN peacekeepers in April 1992. That's what I consider to be the start of the logical progression of a primarily policing-type approach which led, in just a few months' time, to a disastrous escalation.

Alright, but sometimes the police can be useful! What do you think should have been done?

Of course, but it was the Somali police force that had to be reconstituted. That was what the US aid coordinator, Andrew Natsios, suggested; he envisioned reinstating 2,400 of the 3,500 members of what had been the national police force. In his view, those older men—who were still respected in the country because they had to some extent escaped Siad Barre's control while he was in power—could begin serving again, provided they got active support. But that assumed a willingness to rely on Somali society—a willingness that was apparently not shared, as foreign troops were entrusted with what would then become an impossible task.

Some of us, including Natsios, also proposed a complementary, non-policing approach to security, based on the observation that the scarcity of food and uncertainty about its arrival were major contributors to insecurity. For that reason, and because we knew it was possible to find a compromise with the leadership of the factions, we suggested doing things on a much larger scale, to try to saturate the market with basic foodstuffs in order to drive down their value and thus the benefits of diverting them. We also stressed the importance of regular, predictable deliveries, in order to alleviate tensions and discourage hoarding. I still believe it was worth trying. I would add that I don't think that option was rejected out of malice, but out of an inability to think about security outside established, UN-type law-and-order approaches. I don't think we've made any progress in that direction.

What percentage of the food was being diverted? By the way, you seem rather indulgent toward the looters ...

Estimates put the diversions at around 20%–30%, on average, and I hasten to add that that is a very rough approximation. But it's important to know at least the order of magnitude, and it was the diversion figures, together with the mortality figures (both grossly exaggerated), that were the decisive argument for sending an expeditionary force.

Before talking about that, however, I'd like to respond to what you suspect is my indulgence. There were the usual war profiteers, of course, who were already rich and wanted to enrich themselves further; I have absolutely no indulgence toward them. To combat diversion, you have to start by identifying who is instigating the looting. The UN never tried to apply sanctions against these predators. They could have at least tried to convince the supposed political leaders to exercise their authority in this area. If the warlords had any responsibility for it, it was due more to a lack of willingness to control their troops and representatives than to taking part in the attacks themselves. On the other hand, I can't make an overarching moral judgement on the young militiamen who did the looting, because in that context of scarcity it was their job to feed their own. And though part of the food was "diverted" and travelled unorthodox routes, it did reach its target. I think we have to distinguish between predation and unofficial distribution. Hence the fact that I do not see them as enemies of mankind.

So you have more nuanced views on Somalia than the media. Who benefits from such caricatures? Is it ideological blindness? Or do these stereotypes stem from a shared representation in the Western imagination?

The Somali famine hit the front pages in the summer of 1992. CNN had accompanied a US senator to the Kenya–Somalia border, and sent back harrowing pictures of groups of emaciated children. At almost exactly the same time, Bernard Kouchner—France's Minister of Health and Humanitarian Action at the time—was doing the same in Baidoa, the city that was ground zero for the disaster, with Antenne 2 (public TV channel). Somalia then became a TV news story, with the effects one might expect: pressure to act, demonstrate commitment, offer solutions, and use the opportunity for self-promotion. In short, for better or worse, Somalia was put on the agenda, and on the top of the UN's agenda. The United States—followed by France and some other European countries—decided to set up an air bridge to dramatically scale-up the relief effort. Though it came fairly late, after the famine had already done great damage, it was a welcome decision.

But just as the aid was finally being stepped up to meet the needs, signs of a change in direction appeared. In early September, Mohamed Sahnoun—the UN Special Representative for Somalia, who was in the midst of negotiating to send 500 peacekeepers—learned from the BBC that the non-negotiated arrival of 2,500 additional soldiers was imminent. A blunt way of saying that the time for negotiation had passed, and that it was time to use force. Such inadequate force, incidentally, that, once on the ground, the peacekeepers sent to protect the aid had to hire their own guards for protection!

Phase 2 of that strategy: once all talks were halted, there began a media campaign on food theft by armed gangs, culminating in the "news" from the UN Secretary-General that 80% of the aid had been looted. That inflated figure—issued by an office in New York and accepted as fact—played the same role, as a trigger, in Somalia as the lies about Iraqi troops killing babies did in the Gulf crisis. There, too, massive numbers of innocents supposedly being killed needed saving from their executioners.

The Iraqi Army massacring babies? Can you remind me about that episode?

In October 1990, a young Kuwaiti woman testified before the US Congress, describing the atrocities committed by Iraqi soldiers against babies in a hospital where she happened to be. Her testimony made a huge impact, tipping the vote in Congress and precipitating the war. Only later was it learned that her testimony was false, probably dreamed up by a public relations agency hired by the Kuwaiti government in exile with the collaboration of the White House. The young woman, whose identity had been withheld for "security reasons", was in reality the daughter of Kuwait's Ambassador to Washington.[1]

Alright, but then why, in the case of Somalia, was a UN Secretary-General willing to fabricate and spread false information? Did it have to do with his personal ideology?

Boutros Boutros-Ghali, who was elected in December 1991 and was the first African to hold that position, was the first Secretary-General of the post-Cold War period. His plan was to restore the original scope of the UN's mission, and he wanted to make his mark by strengthening the capacity for military and legal intervention set forth in its charter but long held in check by the automatic veto that prevailed during the Cold War. He introduced his plan in June 1992 under the title *An Agenda for Peace*; it focused on multidimensional (diplomatic, economic, humanitarian, military and legal) interventions. And, indeed, more peacekeepers were deployed during his term in office (50,000) than during the previous 45 years of the UN's existence. The scale of the famine, the horrifying images that paraded across TV screens, and the obvious powerlessness of the peacekeepers most likely pushed him to make his plan more radical. I think he wanted to make Somalia the test case for using muscular intervention to restore order and rebuild states; underneath that design lay his ambition to create a permanent UN intervention force. While I'm far from a believer in the utopian idea of liberal interventionism underlying that project, I see no malice there other than arranging the facts to fit the plan.

Please explain that. How can someone arrange facts as he pleases without any malice? Is reality that malleable?

To my mind, Boutros-Ghali had no hidden, dishonourable intentions, but a plan to restore the UN's capacity for action, which the Cold War had neutralized; that's why I chose that turn of phrase. And as we have seen, there was indeed famine, war and aid diversion. What's troubling is that reality alone wasn't seemingly enough to justify such a plan; that it had to be distorted and overdramatized to do so. Because, not content to reverse the proportions of diverted and distributed aid, the Secretary-General's office also took the numbers from

MSF's nutrition survey and extrapolated them to the entire population, though they "only" applied to the internally displaced people. And they used those numbers to claim that an entire generation of young Somalis was on the verge of disappearing.

And those lies, or exaggerations, were enough to trigger the intervention?

No. There again, we find a confluence of desires and circumstances. The latter included the displaced populations overwhelming Somalia's neighbours, among them Ethiopia, with which it had fought. In UN lingo this constituted a "threat to the peace", covered by Chapter VII of the UN Charter, which allows for the sending of offensive armed forces. As the situation in Somalia deteriorated further, that muscular intervention I was talking about required a real military force—not the contingents of Blue Helmets equipped, at best, for self-defence, still poorly coordinated, and responsible for keeping a nonexistent peace. In that context, only the US Army would be enough, and so Boutros-Ghali turned to Washington. The US was still basking in its military and political victory in the Near East after "liberating" Kuwait, and was seen as master of the world thanks to the implosion of the USSR, which had proved incapable of opposing America's plan at the UN.

Operation Desert Storm was supposed to usher in a new era in international relations, now under the banner of law rather than force. At least that was what George Bush declared on the day Allied troops went to war. But there was a strong whiff of oil hovering over that operation, and of US strategic interests more broadly. Intervening to help starving Somali children could have been a way to demonstrate the benevolent—and in this instance selfless—nature of American power. The announcement was made on 24 November, Thanksgiving Eve—a good time, like Christmas, to celebrate human solidarity—and was very well-received by the American public. A grand exit for a president who, despite his victory in Iraq, had just lost the election to Bill Clinton. And it must have been especially tempting to restore his moral image with a rescue operation whose aftermath his rival and successor would have to deal with.

In your publication *Somalia: A Humanitarian Crime*,[2] you describe the spectacular landing of American troops in Mogadishu (Somalia's capital), and the outcome of that adventure, which was not exactly glorious.

Yes, the launch of Operation Restore Hope on 9 December was an enormous spectacle, designed and choreographed for prime-time television in the US. An enormous cargo ship carrying 45,000 tons of supplies and 1,400 vehicles took up almost the entire port of Mogadishu, while the Marines disembarked in military operation-style, wearing face paint and bearing weapons, and hundreds of journalists in shorts and sneakers watched and photographed them. It was pure hype, but whatever. More significant was the first US Army-escorted aid convoy; loaded with 20 tons of food, it left the port a few days later heading north from Mogadishu, escorted like an aircraft carrier with some hundred journalists in its wake. It was an event, presented as a "first". No one, however, paid the slightest attention to the departure of hundreds of tons of food that an old Red Cross-chartered tub unloaded—as it did every week—only 20 kilometres away. Because it was said that no boats could unload without Marine protection, it didn't exist. Only one journalist, *Libération*'s Stephen Smith, covered the non-event, far from the big show.

So, on one hand, we have 20 tons carried to UN warehouses by a heavily armed military convoy, and on the other, 400 tons transferred from a (Mozambican) boat by Somali day labourers and transported by local trucks to the distribution centres I mentioned earlier. True, those truckers had to pay "fees" to the warlords, pay "tolls" at checkpoints, and so put up with having some of their cargo taken, as I said. But those added costs were nothing compared to the cost of militarized transport; those 400 tons from the Red Cross and Red Crescent were obviously infinitely less expensive than the 20 tons from the US Army! Operation Restore Hope cost an estimated billion dollars. If the equivalent of ten dollars' worth of aid distributed by the Red Cross cost two dollars, the same quantity carried by the operation's soldiers must have cost a hundred times more. Not everything is a matter of accounting, it's true, but such orders of magnitude say something about the weakness of the strategy, chosen, once again, for reasons having little to do with the situation. As I said, Somalia was like the story of the sorcerer's apprentice. At least that is how I understand the series of unfortunate decisions that led to the fiasco.

So the media portrayal of the war in Somalia was based on two stereotypes: the all-powerful US leading a coalition of the willing; and Somalia in flames, at the mercy of gangs...

The United States did indeed supply about 30,000 of the 40,000 troops deployed under the aegis of the UN with the mission of saving and pacifying the country. The aid they distributed helped, of course, but it didn't end the famine, as is often said, because it came very late. Most of the victims had already died, and by late 1992 the mortality rate had fallen sharply, from 25 per 10,000 a day during the summer to 5 per 10,000 a day at that point. Though that still exceeded the "emergency threshold",[3] it showed that the famine was abating, after the high initial mortality rate, thanks to the aid that had, in spite of everything, arrived over the previous months. The fireman had arrived on the scene, it's true, but after the house had burned down almost completely. They put out the last few flames, but it was nothing to crow about. I should add, however, that many Somalis and humanitarian organizations—including MSF, of course—initially welcomed the new operation with joy, seeing it, despite everything, as a response to the insecurity and looting. While their joy didn't last long, it served as a reminder of how many believed in the ability of military power to bring peace. While December 1992 was a triumphant moment for the US and proponents of humanitarian military intervention, almighty America would quickly become disillusioned, and with it those who had placed their hopes in a virtuous use of armed force.

I won't go into detail about the sometimes baroque decisions and tragic miscalculations that led to the fiasco, which I described in *Somalia: A Humanitarian Crime*.[4] I'll only talk about the Americans' rapidly launched search for weapons, because it encapsulates the various aspects of the crisis. While one side considered it a means of "pacification", the other side saw it as a personal threat and a violation of sovereignty. To that contradiction I would add the fact, rarely mentioned, that many of the people tracking down weapons owners in Mogadishu would have risked their lives to stop someone from taking away the weapons they kept at home in the United States. What they considered a constitutional right at home was a crime to be put right in Somalia. It was, obviously, equally unacceptable to the Somalis, whether they were members of the warring factions or not, and that effort contributed to both the militaristic turn that international operations took and the growing hostility to them.

From misunderstandings to provocations, the US–UN troops gradually became just another de facto clan, losing control of their actions and viewed by most Somalis as an occupying force. Not wanting his troops to get bogged down, Clinton was looking for a political outcome that would allow him to order a dignified withdrawal. Hence the plan to capture Aidid, who had emerged in the meantime as the leading opponent of the US presence. A manhunt—with a bounty on the "wanted" person's head—was launched after 24 Pakistani soldiers died in a tense ambush. That sequence of events would end on 3 October with a disastrous commando raid against Aidid. Eighteen Rangers and 500 Somalis were killed, a pilot was taken prisoner, and some soldiers were lynched and dragged through the streets. It was a terrible, humiliating scene, images of which were seen around the world. As a result, Clinton decided to end American involvement in Somalia. The last US troops quietly left the country on 25 March 1994, and the UN troops followed a year later.

So, to sum up, the war in Somalia was conducted for the wrong reasons and in disastrous fashion?

That's right. The operation was not only based on misleading simplifications, sidelining Somali society, and false allegations; it was also given the grandiose task of "pacification" and rebuilding the state. Whatever one might think about the course events would have taken without this "humanitarian war", which we obviously cannot know, one thing seems certain: that having been launched under such inauspicious circumstances, it couldn't help failing. And in so doing, it made worse the very situation it hoped to improve.

4

KOSOVO

A MORALLY JUSTIFIED UNJUST WAR?

The specialists may have learned their lesson from the war in Somalia, but that didn't prevent other "humanitarian" armed interventions … like the one in Kosovo. Were all these interventions comparable?

Operation Restore Hope is generally cited more as an object lesson than as an example to be followed, since no one really disputes that the operation was a failure. The 1990s were the heyday of UN interventionism, as I said, with an unprecedented increase in military operations in Liberia and Sierra Leone, Haiti, Cambodia, the former Yugoslavia, Rwanda and Angola, just to mention the largest ones. Their missions were varied, from monitoring a ceasefire to protecting an elected government, including observing or consolidating a political transition. Their methods also varied, from simply documenting agreement violations or atrocities to the direct exercise of force, as was the case, for example, with Nigeria's armed forces (under the UN flag) in Sierra Leone.

Each situation should be judged on its own merits, but whatever one thinks about the results of UN operations, we have to recognize that the decision to launch them relied on acknowledged facts. Yet that was not the case with Kosovo, where the war began in a climate of intense propaganda based on allegations of massacre and even genocide. That said, the geography of Kosovo—a small territory in Europe—placed the question in a different political perspective—one in which the consequences of the war, whose successful outcome was conceivable from the outset, could be handled by those conducting it. Or, in the language of just war theory, it was not unreasonable to think that there were real "chances of success". That's one of the reasons I approved of it despite the lies used to justify it, unlike the wars we have just discussed at some length.

What was the other reason—aside from the real chance of success—prompting you in the beginning to support the war in Kosovo?

The other reason was Slobodan Milošević's regime, which relied on fascistic paramilitary groups, which had already committed mass atrocities in Bosnia and Kosovo. Milošević had begun to redraw the borders of the former Yugoslavia along ethnic lines using violence—a project that European nations had decided to banish from the continent in the wake of World War II. The repression by Belgrade and its militias of the armed insurrection begun in 1997 was extremely harsh, and the massacres in Bosnia were a precedent portending further violence.

Can you remind us about the complex, long-standing context in which the war began?

Kosovo was where the unrest in the former Yugoslavia began, in 1980–1, after Tito's death in 1980. It voted for independence in a secretly held referendum in 1991, when the fighting in Croatia was just beginning. Yet the referendum wasn't mentioned in the Dayton Accords (21 November 1995) ending the Bosnian War, thus helping to delegitimize Kosovo's president, Ibrahim Rugova, a long-time opponent of Belgrade and professed pacifist. Perhaps history would have taken a different course had the man some called the "Gandhi of Kosovo" been given the European support he no doubt deserved. Why didn't that happen? I don't know. But it was a new opposition group, the Kosovo Liberation Army (KLA), which rose up against Milošević in 1996 and came to power at the end of the 1999 war.

As outlined, that chronology seems to suggest that Europe preferred armed confrontation and so "fabricated" the war in Kosovo ... You wouldn't go that far, however, would you?

I have asked myself that question, but have no answer, perhaps for lack of precise enough knowledge of the history. I usually make an effort to distinguish between a series of events and a causal chain, so that I'm not tempted, as in this case, to be too hasty in my conclusions. On the other hand, given the unacceptable conditions it imposed on Milošević, beginning with a series of "non-negotiable" principles, I think the Rambouillet Conference (February–March 1999) was used by the United States as a diplomatic façade behind which the war plan came together. Although president in name, the pacifist Rugova had been kept out of the conference in favour of KLA leader Hashim Thaçi, a military man. Kissinger himself considered the conditions unacceptable: "The Rambouillet text, which called on Serbia to admit NATO troops throughout Yugoslavia, was a provocation, an excuse to start bombing. Rambouillet is not a document that an angelic Serb could have accepted. It was a terrible diplomatic document that should never have been presented in that form."[1] He might have added that it was primarily the American side— represented by Madeleine Albright—that was pushing things to extremes; Hubert Védrine of France and Robin Cook of Britain took a position much more open to Serbian expectations.

By that I mean that the Americans wanted the war for American reasons. Just as they intervened to end the Bosnian war with the Dayton Accords, on this occasion they were reaffirming their status as a military power in Europe through NATO. That doesn't mean that they provoked the war, but that they wanted to exploit it for their own purposes. While for some people that imperial aim was sufficient reason to oppose the war, for others— who considered it very real—it was not a decisive argument, given the Serbian violence on the ground.

Are you saying that it was NATO propaganda, in a way, that started the war? Isn't that a bit of an exaggeration?

The propaganda started before, on both sides, but 1999 began with the very real death of 45 Kosovar Albanians, killed by the Serbian police in Račak. Was it a massacre or an armed confrontation? Very likely a massacre in retaliation for previous killings. But the village was very likely harbouring some KLA fighters, who were shot. That massacre led to negotiations that NATO framed as a last chance—a sort of elaborate ultimatum. Two weeks later, just before the Rambouillet Conference started, NATO authorized its Secretary-General, Javier Solana, to begin airstrikes if necessary. Given the back-and-forth and twists and turns of the conference (6 February— 19 March), we can assume that not all of the "Allies", as they called themselves, were on the same page. Yet the fact remains that NATO declared war on 24 March, shortly after the German Defence Minister revealed that there was a plan, called Operation Horseshoe, which Milošević's Serbian forces had been developing since 1998 to trap Kosovo's Albanian population in a vice-like movement and push them out of the province. So the source of that "information" was not NATO itself, but the German government, no doubt anxious to justify its participation in the war to a very divided public. It was also a windfall for the Americans at a time when hundreds of thousands of Albanians were fleeing the war in Kosovo. Labelled a genocide and accompanied by rumours of large-scale massacres, Operation Horseshoe helped stifle any questions about the intervention and elevated its status to a rescue operation. And the exodus of some 700,000 Albanians to Macedonia, Montenegro and Albania was only too real, lending credence to the accusations that there was a terrorist plan in action.

Do you dispute the genocidal intentions of the Serbs in Kosovo? Why, then, the exodus?

It was some German officers themselves who disputed it, notably in *Der Spiegel*. Operation Horseshoe was a pure creation of the special services at the request of Defence Minister Rudolf Scharping; there is no debate about that. What is less clear to me, and difficult to determine in any case, is what caused the mass exodus. NATO attributed it to organized Serb paramilitary actions, and opponents blamed it on the "Allied" bombing, using the calendar to back up their claim, since the bulk of the exodus occurred while the bombs were falling. NATO argued that the population movements had started prior to the war.

What do you think? Was the Albanian exodus caused by Serb paramilitaries or by NATO?

Though there are contradictory intentions underlying those assertions, they are not mutually exclusive. It is plausible that the paramilitaries' atrocities caused some portion of the population to flee, while another portion was fleeing the bombs. And while the opponents' theory was apparently closer to the truth, that in no way negates the atrocities, the Serb paramilitaries' policy of terror, or the active support they were getting from Belgrade. As I said, those were the reasons—that is, the regime and the methods it had already used in Bosnia, together with the feasibility of decent post-intervention management—that led me to support the war. That hundreds of thousands of Kosovars fled the NATO bombings, which may well have been the case, doesn't change my opinion, and in particular—and this is not just a detail—because it didn't turn the Kosovar Albanian population against the people sending the bombs.

Moreover, the loss of human life was far less than what had been predicted before hostilities started and just after they began. The warmongers talked about hundreds of thousands of Kosovar victims, already killed or about to be killed by the Serbian forces, and then lowered that to tens of thousands without any more convincing evidence. The NGOs, the International Criminal Court and the Red Cross attempted to provide counts and estimates of the number of dead, which ranged widely from 3,000 to 13,400 dead, depending on the period in question and the methods used, with approximately 500 of those deaths caused by NATO bombing. Now that I know—in hindsight and with information gleaned from various sources—that NATO and the US were pushing for war, I'm torn. Was the other principle I consider fundamental—that is, the use of violence as a last resort—respected? I have my doubts, and that makes me more circumspect today than I was at the time. I am not, however, going back on my positions.

In April 1999 you signed a group op-ed in *Libération* supporting the Kosovo Liberation Army (KLA), an anti-Milošević paramilitary

organization. Yet that movement had some pretty unsavoury politics.

You're right. The KLA, which was created in 1991, was an umbrella organization of small groups of Albanian-style Marxist-Leninists and ultranationalists. It funded itself by means of a "revolutionary tax" and drug trafficking, among other things, and had a mix of radical ideologies and violent practices that do not generally bode well at all. In addition, having been the victim of injustice is no guarantee of one's becoming the incarnation of justice, and we have seen many cases where the oppressed turn into oppressors.

I don't think, now, that the KLA was all that much better than the Serbian ultranationalist groups it was fighting, but it was well regarded for its role in the resistance to Belgrade and enjoyed popular support. In politics—and in collective action in general—we don't always get things right at the beginning, and I've made a lot of mistakes in my public life. That being said, I continue to stand by the spirit of that op-ed piece, which advocated supporting the KLA so that Kosovars could have a role in freeing themselves from oppression, as opposed to waiting for someone else to come and save them. It seemed to me that, inasmuch as the Serbian government had chosen violent confrontation, the KLA was the lesser evil because limiting its power once the war was won seemed possible. In the meantime, however, the disparity in military strength made support for them necessary. It would have been far better to give Ibrahim Rugova the international presence he lacked at the time of the Dayton Accords, but that was not done.

A few years later, it was too late; the KLA had claimed the mantle of Kosovar representative, and that was the context in which the choice had to be made.

You say that the war in Kosovo was based on a lie and that you no longer believe that war was a last resort. After criticism like that, can we still call it a "just war"?

Before labelling it, let's remember that the war, which began on 24 March, ended on the following 8 June, when Milošević accepted the peace plan—an agreement in which Russian mediation was essential. A Russian contingent, symbolic in number, had entered the capital, Pristina, just a few days ahead of NATO troops. In early July the UN named Bernard Kouchner the head of the United Nations Interim Administration Mission in Kosovo (UNMIK); he would serve as the proconsul for the new UN protectorate of Kosovo for 18 months. After that, the KLA took the helm and in 2008 declared the province independent, with support from NATO members but against China's and Russia's wishes and so without Security Council recognition.

That clarified, I'll get to your question, to which I'll add that the war was declared by NATO, in violation of international law, and so failed to meet another important legal criterion. The UN legalized the operation retroactively, as it did after the Iraq invasion, which it had condemned in 2003. Unlike the Libyan and Somali cases we just looked at, however, it was a dangerous situation, punctuated in 1998–9 by serious incidents, that could possibly be remedied by creating a new situation through force. In the same way, I—along with many others—thought that Europe should have helped the Bosnians militarily during the Bosnian War, rather than imposing an embargo that penalized both aggressors and their victims, and sending only food and medicine.

Obviously, the Kosovo War did not meet the "just war" criteria as we described them; first, because we failed to try everything to avoid it, and second, because it was not decided by a legitimate authority (the Russians opposed it in the Security Council). But one might reasonably have thought it would put an end to the killing and the anti-Albanian apartheid, and allow the creation of a controllable, if not democratic, government in a territory the size of two French departments. The result has not, in fact, been all that inspiring. Kosovo does not have a viable economy, and has become a sort of NATO barracks led by people with strong mobster tendencies, from which Serbs have been driven out or relegated to enclaves, along with most of the Roma, under the indifferent eyes of NATO troops. It survives, miserably, on EU subsidies, despite the fact that it has not been recognized by certain EU countries like Spain, Cyprus and others, which have little intention of recognizing the independence of a province that gained it against central government opposition.

If numerous commentators are to be believed, however, the Kosovo War was a step forward for the right to humanitarian intervention.

A place where intervention happened, without a doubt. Was it the manifestation of a right to armed intervention in the making? One could say that, and it was exactly what supporters of the "right" to intervene did say on seeing its triumphant return when the UN adopted the "Responsibility to Protect". I should note, in passing, that the members of the Commission on Intervention and State Sovereignty, which we have talked about, were working on the "R2P" report during the Kosovo operation and that the operation probably played some part in their discussions and final recommendations. Some analysts dispute that there's a connection between the right and duty to intervene, as promoted by Bernard Kouchner and the jurist Mario Bettati, and the R2P, as adopted by the UN.[2] While it was Kofi Annan, of course, who shepherded the idea through the complex maze at the UN and presented it to the Security Council, I think Kouchner and Bettati can rightfully claim their share of the author's rights.

Don't the liberties Western democracies take with the facts to justify war show their authoritarian temptations?

In Somalia, as in Kosovo, we missed an opportunity to try to improve a crisis situation through peaceful means. Both of those "humanitarian wars", bookends to the post-Cold War decade, were presented as last-chance rescue operations, and that's how the decision to go to war in Libya was characterized as well. Admittedly, amplification and distortion of the facts was a trait that all three wars shared, but one might argue that propaganda accompanies all wars. Democracies and dictatorships are not, in fact, all that different when it comes to the relationship with the truth in war situations—with the possible caveat that democracies tend to appeal to morality, while dictatorships invoke security or sovereignty. For the latter, I'm thinking of Chechnya, Syria and Yemen, in particular, but also of course the "war on terror", where US democracy is showing its true face— that is, the dictatorial leanings of the American empire.

5

AFGHANISTAN AND IRAQ

TWO WARS "FOR CIVILIZATION"

The Americans led another "moral" war in Afghanistan. Perhaps we should distinguish between the various phases of that conflict?

Indeed. It was hard to argue with the United States' initial response after the September 11 attacks, because an attack like that cannot go unanswered. No one really challenged it, in any case, except perhaps in a marginal way. But two objectives were mixed up at the outset: overthrowing the Taliban regime in Kabul, and destroying al-Qaeda training camps. The terrorist organization, a legitimate target, was wrongly identified with the Afghan government—which, though it did allow al-Qaeda to set up shop in the country, was not involved in the attacks. The Afghan Taliban—which is not a political party but a kind of relatively diversified front—are nationalists, first and foremost. Islamic nationalists, admittedly, but not international jihadists. They do use terrorism, that's indisputable, but only within their own borders and against an identified local enemy. Their alliance with al-Qaeda dates back to the war of resistance against the Red Army in the 1980s—a time when they were, if you recall, supported by the United States, as was Bin Laden's group, when he had an "in" at the Pentagon. America was not an enemy of al-Qaeda until it established military bases in Saudi Arabia in the context of the 1991 Gulf War. The Taliban, which was in power in Kabul from 1995 to 2001 after defeating other Afghan factions—the one led by Commander Massoud, in particular—was very much accepted by Washington.

During the first phase, an international law enforcement operation in 2001–2, American forces destroyed a substantial portion of al-Qaeda's infrastructure in Afghanistan. Although they missed Bin Laden, they were able to hunt for him using law enforcement methods, as pointed out by the many politicians and specialists criticizing the very notion of a "war on terror" at that time. And as you no doubt remember, the US Department of Defense dubbed the operation "Operation Infinite Justice", before renaming it "Operation Enduring Freedom". After a start like that, it's no surprise that what followed looked like a war for civilization.

But how did the hunt for al-Qaeda leaders turn into a "war for civilization"?

The Taliban fell five weeks after the offensive began and an interim government led by Hamid Karzai was installed in late 2001. Foreign forces could have begun to withdraw at that point, leaving the Afghan people to find their own political solution, but the opposite occurred. Foreign contingents were beefed up, NATO was deployed under the appellation ISAF (International Security and Assistance Force), and the magical concepts that had emerged in the 1990s arrived in force, with state-building, confidence-building, nation-building, peace-building and so on. Roads, bridges and schools were built, young people trained, and hospitals renovated. That's what NATO and the coalition countries highlight, and it's beyond dispute. NGOs were soon enlisted (unbeknown to themselves) in that coalition, attracted by the special funding available, it's true, but also by a sense of being useful to people who were suffering enormously. The pacificatory expeditionary force continued to grow throughout the decade, creating a flourishing market for private security companies. But it was no obstacle to the Taliban's seemingly inexorable advance. The numerous military "blunders" and hundreds of resulting deaths, the colonialist behaviour, the onerous American tutelage, the double-dealing of Pakistan and Saudi Arabia, the pervasive corruption, and the hostility created everywhere by the continuing presence of foreign armies, are enough to explain the success of the Islamist rebellion. The TV series *Kaboul Kitchen*[1] was an accurate portrayal of humanitarian expat life in Kabul and of the colonial atmosphere in which everyone in that world—humanitarian workers, consultants, civilian members of the various international organizations, and mercenaries—lived, all of them well aware that ultimately, in one way or another, the Taliban would return to power.

How, specifically, did the US government get France to agree to the war, in a context of likely defeat and military deaths—90 thus far?

Women's rights became a favourite rationalization over the course of time. In the early 2000s, the intellectual and political context was suddenly (re)polarized by a new global enemy, jihadism, amplified by the fallout from the Second Intifada (2000–5) and the very bitter tensions it provoked. In France there were fiery debates over the "veil" and "Islam and the Republic", with the September 11 attacks as a backdrop. The secular Republic—as defended by Sarkozy, Hollande and then Prime Minister Valls, along with numerous intellectuals and editorial writers—conveniently united the fight against Islamist obscurantism in France with that in Afghanistan. It was a matter of liberating women from their "cloth prison"—an oft-used expression—while fighting for our security against terrorism. Another double "brainwashing".

However, it was politically and militarily impossible to replicate the Kosovo model in a country with 34 million people, larger than France, that had successfully resisted foreign occupation since the nineteenth century. And it goes without saying that no one in Afghanistan was attempting to free women from their veils; it would take more than ISAF soldiers to get the women wearing a veil or burka to throw off their "cloth chains".

Was France a participant in this moral crusade to impose Western values by force?

In a word, yes. France's military involvement—intended primarily, it seems to me, to please our US allies so they would forgive our opposition to the invasion of Iraq—had to be cloaked in other, more saleable, virtues. There was security, of course, but the Taliban posed no credible threat to France or to Europe. More was needed, and the unifying theme of "France's universal values"—the values it's up to us to share and spread throughout the world—fitted the bill. What better expression of those than the condition of women, a marker of choice that encompasses all the other claims of civilization, and internationally monitored elections, the usual sign of peaceful political practice?

Nicolas Sarkozy illustrated the barbaric treatment of women in several interviews, claiming that women wearing nail polish were having their arms cut off by the Taliban. I don't know where he got that story, since no one ever asked him—in any of the interviews I saw, in any case. But the moment I heard it, it reminded me of General Westmoreland's claims during the Vietnam War that the Viet Cong were cutting off the arms of children vaccinated by the US Army. The French accused the Germans of something similar during World War I, but few were apparently struck by that similarity, either, and despite the hyperbole—"Do you want someone cutting off your wife's or daughter's arm? I don't!"—the story was taken at face value. Journalists and legislators were rightly worried about the stalemate and losses, and more generally about the impasse in which the foreign forces found themselves, but they seemed ignorant of the fact that even that final justification for our presence was based only on a worn-out piece of propaganda. You probably remember the *Time* magazine cover—it was in August 2010 and made a big splash—showing a young woman whose nose had been cut off, leaving a gaping hole in the centre of her beautiful face, with the caption "What Happens If We Leave Afghanistan". Aisha, age 18, became the symbol of Islamic brutality that had to be stopped, at a time when people were questioning, in the US as well, the prospect of the longest military engagement in the country's history. The Taliban denied having committed the act, which they condemned in no uncertain terms and blamed on a violent husband, while the article claimed it was a sentence from an Islamic court. Believe them or not, the fact is that it happened while American troops were in the country, once again proving that appealing to emotion at least momentarily obviates the need to be coherent.

Walking such a fine line isn't easy; on one side, criticizing Western lies, and, on the other, acknowledging the Taliban's terrible violence.

I'm obviously not arguing with the fact that women are oppressed in Afghanistan, but rather with using it to justify our military presence, as if military power was a response to male violence. Moreover, the Taliban didn't hold up the madman who committed that despicable crime as a model, even had he been one of theirs, which we don't know.

I think it's completely reasonable to use the condition of women—and gay people, as well—as a marker of democracy, provided it is applied everywhere. Would we consider invading India, or imposing sanctions on it, on the grounds that it's one of the most dangerous countries in the world for women, with its female infanticide, forced marriage, dowry crimes and rape? In Mexico, mass killings, sex crimes and mutilation of women have all reached frightening proportions since the cartel wars began, but no one would think of sending an expeditionary force there to sort things out. I should point out, in passing, that the war on drugs is now increasingly being blamed for the terrifying proliferation of gangs in Central America, just as prohibition gave rise to gangs in 1920s America. There again, we see that military force is useless for anything except fighting another army!

The fact remains that people never talk about violence against women as much as when it happens in a Muslim country. And yet we treat these issues differently when they occur in countries that are allies, like Saudi Arabia and the other Gulf countries, or in conflict situations like Iran and Afghanistan. In France, a woman is killed by her spouse every three days, and there are tens of thousands of rapes each year, yet we don't blame such horrors on our country's dominant Catholic culture.

In the words of La Fontaine, "Depending on whether you are mighty or in lack, the court will judge you white or black". And depending, we might add, on whether you are friend or enemy. But is there a total disconnect between the moral justification for the war and its true political reasons?

Yes, I think the fundamental reason why France got involved—and not just France—was to be at the Americans' side. Political analyst Bertrand Badie showed how France became pro-NATO after the Iraq War, at the G8 in Evian in June 2003, a move that started with Chirac and continued with his successors. He blamed it on France's fear—which he considered overblown—of US economic and political retaliation for its opposition to the Iraq War in 2003. It was to demonstrate our solidarity with the US through action, even if it meant getting bogged down in what was quickly becoming an absurd war. But since those were not convincing enough reasons for the public, whose support is required in a democracy, an incontrovertible moral justification had to be given. Nothing new there; brainwashing is part and parcel of modern warfare, so we're on familiar ground. What strikes me, and concerns me—in this case as in the previous ones we've discussed—is the warm reception that propaganda received or, put another way, the ease with which we still divide the world into civilized and barbarian, into "us" and "them".

The *Arrêt sur images* website[2] compared the media treatment of the war in Afghanistan to its treatment of the first phase of the Algerian War of Independence (1954–9), when the latter was being fought only in the *maquis*—and not the urban areas, where it was concentrated in the second phase. There is a common theme: the West's war against terrorism and the civilizing role of France; we see no images from the opposing camp. We see the "convert", the one who changed sides, the ex-Fellagha or ex-Taliban who chose civilization and peace. Let me qualify that remark by noting that move-ments in the opposite direction, from the Afghan army to the Taliban, were not concealed. And the last, but not least, similarity: the French public's awareness that the country was at war began with the August 2008 ambush in the Uzbin Valley (where 10 French soldiers and their Afghan interpreter were killed), as it did with the May 1956 Ambush of Palestro (when 19 French soldiers were killed).

But when you think about the logic behind these moral wars, about wanting to create a state *ex nihilo*, about wanting to impose an ideology with little regard for reality, all via a strong army and waging war ... doesn't that reflect a problem in terms of democracy as well? Can a true democracy behave like that? Political jour-nalists in the mainstream media fail to point out contradictions in speeches or identify ideo-logical problems; often, they shut up altogether with an all-powerful head of state. Isn't that a failure of democracy as well?

No doubt, but in the sense that a hospital-acquired infec-tion is a failure by the hospital, or in the sense of *pharma-kon*, where remedy and poison are inextricably linked. Democracy is precious because it's a political system that incorporates the idea of its own imperfection, and thus the utility of criticism. But as Tzvetan Todorov shows in his recent book,[3] that fundamental property is not all there is to democracy. He starts from the observation that the constant movement brought about by the desire

for perfectibility makes progress a fundamental component of the democratic ideal. Hence, he tells us, the
messianic temptation that drives it, because that good—
progress, democracy and civilization—must be shared,
if necessary by pressure and armed force, when circumstances permit. Todorov considers such messianism a
threat that democracy secretes against itself (hence my
pharmakon analogy). He views neo- or ultraliberalism as
the other threat, one that stems from the value democracy attaches to individual freedom. So I'll let Todorov
answer your question. I will simply note that democratic
countries that make freedom of thought and moderation
the bedrock of their collective values, and pluralistic
societies that can boast a well-established tradition of
election and revocation of power, are not necessarily
immune to collective excess. Marc Bloch spoke of World
War I as "an immense experiment in social psychol-
ogy",[4] and like him we might note that fake news can
only survive "on one condition: that it finds a favourable
cultural broth". "In it," he adds, "people unconsciously
express all their prejudices, hatreds, fears, all of their
strong emotions." Again, unique—and therefore unpredictable—circumstances are always required in order for
those emotions to result in decisions as grave as going to
war. In passing, let's put to rest the cliché that democracies are by definition peaceable and dictatorships warlike, and note that there are warlike democracies and
peaceable dictatorships (at least in their relationships
with their neighbours).

**While Marc Bloch studied false news in war-
time, we were dealing with far more than that**

with the supposed WMD: an enormous lie of international proportions. I find it astonishing that the vast majority of the Western world swallowed a lie like that.

No, the entire Western world—the entire world, in fact—denied it. You have to remember the protests all over the world, and in Western Europe in particular. Not always for the right reasons, at first, if you think about international polling showing that more than half of the world's population thought that the September 11 attacks were a CIA fabrication. But the propaganda worked admirably in the United States, where 80% of the population supported the "pre-emptive war" against a "new Hitler".

That said, the war—whose disastrous repercussions we're still living with today—would not have been possible without Prime Minister Tony Blair's "I'll be with you, whatever" promise to George W. Bush, against the advice of the British people who, like the French and other Europeans, were opposed to it. Echoing the WMD theme, he reported having "information" that Iraq could deploy those WMD within 45 minutes, which made neutralizing them seem like an emergency. The UK sent 45,000 soldiers to Iraq, a significant military contribution, and made the war politically feasible by ending US isolation on the issue. I would also note that as with Libya, the British Parliament conducted a lengthy investigation and in 2016 published an extremely detailed report (over 6,400 pages) highly critical of Britain's involvement in Iraq. We're still waiting for its French counterpart to do the same for France's military engagements! Blair was profoundly shaken by this, however, and responded to the criticism by defending his decision: "I believe we made the right decision and the world is better and safer …"

Precisely. And have moral wars based on lies made the world any safer? I'm not sure about that …

It all gave rise to violent, radical movements, some of them—al-Qaeda and the Islamic State—spilling over borders, others remaining within their borders but becoming more radical. In Afghanistan, the Red Army caused the rise of the Taliban and al-Qaeda; Iraq's 1980 attack radicalized the "Islamic Revolution" in Iran; and the 2003 invasion of Iraq led to the creation of the Islamic State. I can't help thinking that the world would be safer had those responsible for its safety—I'm speaking, ironically of course, about the permanent members of the Security Council—not charged headlong into these foolhardy ventures. As we speak [in August 2017], Donald Trump is announcing an increase in American troop levels in Afghanistan, where 31,000 Afghan civilians and 2,400 American soldiers have died since October 2001—an appalling toll, in addition to 20,000 wounded and nearly a trillion dollars spent. While I am sure that Trump couldn't care less about the "just war" doctrine, this does show that a war that could be initially labelled a "just" response to aggression was continued under another pretext—that is, "civilization".

6

INTERNATIONAL HUMANITARIAN LAW

LEGAL PIPE DREAM AND THE LANGUAGE OF POWER

Doesn't your critique of "just", or "moral" and "humanitarian", wars also apply to international humanitarian law? Where does the latter come from? Is it also steeped in ideology?

The "just war" concept aims to limit a ruler's ability to wage war and restrict the means used, as I said at the start of our conversation. From the outset it has incorporated the notion of "proportionality" used by contemporary international humanitarian law (*jus in bello*), and has long introduced the idea that war should be conducted in accordance with the principles of mercy, or the principles of humanity, to use more modern terminology. That is what the most well-known and central component of humanitarian law—the Geneva Conventions—is all about.

But mercy and humanity are obviously not timeless concepts or sentiments, traversing the centuries unchanged, which is why humanitarian law—born in 1864 with the adoption of the First Geneva Convention—needs to be considered within a historical context. Especially since, if humanitarian workers and journalists are to be believed, this law and its underlying principles have been steadily eroding since the Cold War ended.

Let's start with the First Geneva Convention, which was signed on 22 August 1864; it does not mention the word "humanitarian". As its title implies, it deals with "the amelioration of the condition of the wounded in armies in the field" and is broken down into ten articles occupying two pages. It actually contains two, and only two, points. First, it endeavoured to ensure that the sick and wounded were recognized as neutral—that is, off limits to hostilities—along with all that was necessary to their care, that is, health care personnel, ambulances, hospitals, and so on. Second, it introduced a "distinctive and uniform flag", an emblem shared by all nations, bearing a red cross against a white background, as well as an armband for "neutral" personnel bearing that same emblem—based on the Swiss flag, in homage to the country hosting the conference. The Convention has evolved, filling out with each successive conference, and its scope has been broadened to include the wounded and shipwrecked (1906), prisoners (1929), and civilian populations (1949). "Additional protocols" were adopted in 1977 to cover conflicts involving "irregular" forces in domestic conflicts, in the wake of the wars of decolonization and the Vietnam War. It has grown from the original ten articles of the first convention to 559 articles in the convention currently in force. In other words, the military legal experts employed by an increasing number of armies have material that lends itself to all sorts of readings, as was pointed out to me one day by a seasoned delegate of the International Committee of the Red Cross (ICRC), a proponent of simplifying what should be a "code for humanity in war".

But getting back to the origins of humanitarian law, how is the "principle of humanity" underpinning it related to a nineteenth-century conception of war?

There is an inherent paradox, or rather asynchronicity, in that principle, which tells us something of the difficulties in applying it even well before what have been described as more serious and more frequent contemporary violations. In fact, humanitarian law belongs to an old normative framework—the distinction between combatants and non-combatants—and to the singular historical context of nineteenth-century conflicts, of which the Battle of Solferino is the epitome. That battle, in northern Italy, was between a Franco-Sardinian coalition, led by Napoleon III, and the Austrian Army, led by Emperor Franz Joseph. There, in 1859, took place one of the bloodiest clashes since the end of the Napoleonic Wars, leaving more than 30,000 dead and wounded on the battlefield in a single day of fighting. Henry Dunant, a Swiss citizen who was trying to get in contact with Napoleon III to request a concession in Algeria, discovered the battlefield and the dying, a spectacle that shocked the fervent Evangelical (he was one of the founders of the Young Men's Christian Association, later known as the YMCA). Dunant took an active part in organizing first aid for the wounded, whatever their nationality, and later wrote an account of the battle, celebrating the battlefield exploits of the combatants but depicting in unvarnished detail the appalling condition of the casualties left behind.

His book, *A Memory of Solferino*, which he published in 1862 and called his "humanitarian manifesto", was a success in Europe and led to the founding of the International Committee for Relief to the Wounded in 1863. Ten years later, that committee would become the International Committee of the Red Cross, and ultimately spawn national Red Cross societies in every country in the world (there are currently 194 of them). Their first initiative, which began in 1864, was a diplomatic conference for "the amelioration of the condition of the wounded in armies in the field", known as the First Geneva Convention. Less than two years had elapsed between the publication of *A Memory* and the conference; in other words, conditions were favourable in both the halls of power and public opinion. Imperial France seemed particularly open to the project—a reminder that the terms were negotiated by plenipotentiaries of the various signatory countries, alongside generals, and it was not just the work of philanthropists. We will have reason to come back to this point later.

In any case, the asynchronicity of which I spoke lay in the fact that the Battle of Solferino, though a bloodbath, was a battle that took place like a group duel. It was fought far from town, by uniformed combatants; it began at dawn, and ended in the evening when one side was defeated—in this case, the Austrians.

So humanitarian law was invented at a time when the model for war was two opposing armies facing each other on the battlefield, away from towns. How is that a problem?

The paradox of the First Geneva Convention is that it was signed in that context, just when technical developments and political changes were rendering it obsolete. For example, at the time the Geneva Convention was signed, far more powerful weapons, such as machine guns and the first tanks, new logistical resources like trains, and new rifles able to shoot faster and farther were already being used in the American Civil War. That same year, General Sherman—fighting Confederate soldiers supported by a large part of their population—sent his troops on a "march to the sea", giving no quarter, destroying buildings and crops, in order to demoralize the enemy by forcing civilians to bear the burdens of the war. Although the United States was not a party to the First Geneva Convention, it had developed its own *jus in bello*, the Lieber Code, which, while inspired by the same concerns, explicitly gave generals the final say in determining "military necessity".

To take another example, that same doctrine of "military necessity" was used by German commanders to justify the violence with which French irregulars were put down in the Franco-Prussian War, a war in which the notion of a battlefield—and thus the distinction between combatants and non-combatants, and between front and rear—had disappeared. And though Henry Dunant, an admirer of Napoleon III, was in Paris when the regular French army crushed the Paris Commune during the *Semaine Sanglante* (21–28 May 1871), he barely mentioned it in his writings—the man who had been shocked by the carnage in Solferino. Selective indignation has a long history!

The last third of the nineteenth century was also a time of accelerating colonial conquest, "transformed *ipso facto* into just wars in the name of natural law, trade, movement, and property", in the words of historian Enzo Traverso.[1] While humanitarianism by definition refers to a single human species, the concept of the existential equality of all humans is not necessarily included. All humans, but some more than others, as Orwell might say. To take one example: dumdum bullets, prohibited by the Declaration of Saint Petersburg (1868) owing to their "excessive cruelty", were nonetheless permitted for big-game hunting and colonial wars. That distinction was theorized in the language of the time by Gustave Moynier, co-founder and first president of the Red Cross (a position he held for 36 years), who wrote that its founding principles were the product of evangelical morality and civilization. As a result, this progress was "inaccessible to savage tribes that … follow their brutal instincts without a second thought, while civilized nations … seek to humanise it".[2] This proves that humanitarian principles are not immune from the dominant representations of their time, or from political power relationships.

In short, the context in which the 1864 Geneva Convention belonged no longer existed. As a treaty looking toward some mythical nineteenth-century battle was being signed, the conflicts and massacres of civil wars and imperial conquests seem, in retrospect, to foreshadow the total wars of the twentieth century. Henry Dunant himself anticipated the evolution of armed conflict toward total war in a collection of writings published at the end of his life, presciently entitled *L'Avenir sanglant* (The Bloody Future).

There is one aspect of today's wars that existed less at that time, that is, remote warfare, with drones ...

Yes, that has changed things, in so far as the damage from war is more limited—drones don't have much firepower—but the actual theatre of war becomes limitless. As Grégoire Chamayou describes in his theoretical essay on drone warfare,[3] drones can go wherever there are enemies or terrorists (with or without quotation marks). Is he correct in viewing this technology as a fundamental change in how war is conducted, due to the distance between the soldier and his weapon? When the trigger being pressed is thousands of kilometres away from the gun firing the missiles, he writes, the very notion of war disappears, replaced by the hunt, because the reciprocal relationship between the combatants on either side is gone. Is leaving the "reciprocal perceptual field" where combatants used to fight as radical as he says? Was a bomber pilot any closer to his target than his counterpart at the controls of a drone? That's debatable. But what those who promote these weapons claim is that they represent "a major step forward in humanitarian technology".

How cynical. How can a weapon (drones) be presented as a "humanitarian step forward"?

Indeed, the words are cynical but defensible if you look at things from a warfare perspective—which is, remember, where humanitarian law started. Defenders of these weapons compare high-altitude carpet bombing, employed until the 1980s, to the targeted attacks that today's smart weapons make possible. Admittedly, to the hundreds killed "in error" or as "collateral damage" by drones the difference is slim, but drone advocates consider it as deaths avoided.[4] Though this quantitative argument has its limits, there is something to it.

So now you're defending drones? I'm surprised.

No. I'm just agreeing with Dunant here, arguing that if war is inevitable, it should be waged in the least barbarous way—in this case, causing the least number of deaths—possible. But there's more to it than that, because there's another major objection, for which Chamayou's argument is even more convincing, given that killer robot development is in full swing and goes well beyond drones. The total immunity they give their crew, along with the unilateral right to kill, makes war easier, because it is more conceivable than ever in the modern era, in the form of a "hunt without borders". Moreover, the targets of such terrorist hunts are now calculated using pattern-of-life analysis that records and archives movement-tracking and wire-tapping data. Any deviation from usual behaviour becomes suspect. Kill lists are established based on such patterns, among other things. The hunter's target is not necessarily a combatant identified as such, but a suspect—someone who, in a narrow sense, is likely to be an enemy. The scope of action is no longer a geographic area, but the undefined entirety of the world's "high-risk areas".

That is what Obama's Assistant Secretary of Defense, Michael Sheehan, explained at a US Senate hearing in 2013, confirming that for the drones and Special Forces being used to fight against al-Qaeda, the entire world was a battlefield, from Boston to the tribal areas of Pakistan, the Congo and Yemen.[5]

Speaking of technology, I'm thinking of another instrument of death that owes its existence to advanced technology, like killer robots: the DIME bomb. The DIME bomb is considered a "clean" bomb, or was introduced as such by its developer, the US Air Force, thanks to a very small blast radius (only a few metres) combined with high explosive power. As Boris Vian sang in "La Java des bombes atomiques", the only thing that counts is where it falls. How does one get both a small blast radius and high explosive power? Those conflicting constraints were overcome thanks to the fact that instead of spraying shrapnel, the DIME (short for Dense Inert Metal Explosive) bomb produces micro-shrapnel made of tungsten and cobalt, heavy metals whose high initial velocity is slowed by the air after a few metres. Dropped by drones or helicopters, these bombs cause inoperable injuries due to the penetration of undetectable particles, as well as bone and muscle cancers due to the very toxic materials that go into them. While some might find that preferable to the metal barrels filled with explosives and shrapnel that the Syrian army drops from helicopters onto its opponents' neighbourhoods, I personally don't like either one of these appalling weapons. I would be curious to know what the scientists who work on this kind of horror think about when they get up in the morning. That, in any case, is what they call a "clean bomb".

Indeed, we generally blame the people who pull the trigger, but too often forget the scientists who methodically, painstakingly, develop the weapons. Humanitarian law doesn't seem to have anything to say about that.

Indeed. I'm also thinking about another terrifying invention: what the military calls "Lethal Autonomous Weapons Systems", armed devices capable of deciding on their own to take out a target. Several countries—the US in the lead, but also Russia, China and France—are working on it, robot warfare being the model for future wars, according to military leaders. I don't believe the generals' predictions any more than the others, since no one knows what the future will bring, but it's clear that these new weapons already herald a major change in how wars will be fought. Mechanical soldiers that can operate in the air, on the ground and in the water without feeling fatigued or troubled, without emotions or families to compensate—that eliminates a lot of obstacles to their deployment!

The UN created a working group on these questions in 2013; it focuses, in particular, on proliferation issues as well as on the connection with humanitarian law. At least this worrisome development is not being ignored, as the 2015 petition launched by artificial intelligence specialists and renowned researchers like Stephen Hawking and Noam Chomsky again shows. Its signatories expressed their fear of armed conflicts whose scale would be unprecedented and whose time frame would be too short for humans to apprehend. The risk of piracy, which would begin as soon as an object was connected, is yet another worry.

I don't know which weapons will be used in World War III, if it happens, but one thing is certain: World War IV will be fought with clubs, said Albert Einstein, more or less. Let's hope that quip doesn't prove prophetic. In any case, we should note that in the eyes of their promoters, these increasingly "accurate", "surgical" and "smart" weapons are more ethical because they kill fewer humans. As Grégoire Chamayou argues in talking about this topic of "necro-ethics", the more the myth of the ethical robot spreads, the more the moral barriers to deploying killer robots will fall. I was struck by the term "necro-ethics", because the contradiction it suggests—the moralization of killing—has resonances with the objections expressed by opponents of the First Geneva Convention. They saw it as a way to make war "kind", as an attempt to disguise the hell that it is in reality, and thus as a stratagem for rendering it palatable.

Viewed from that angle, humanitarian law can itself be viewed as "necro-ethics", in the sense that it designates who can be eliminated without provoking condemnation, provided one demonstrates a will to spare those protected by humanitarian law.

But you said yourself that you agree with that lesser evil ethic, if I understood you correctly.

That's right. You resign yourself to a lesser evil, that is, to a negative value. I could never have been involved in MSF on a long-term basis if that weren't the case. Nevertheless, I think it's essential to maintain some critical distance with respect to humanitarian law or, more precisely, to the line it draws between lawful and unlawful targets. I'm thinking of the sentiments expressed both publicly and privately by some humanitarians regarding the evolution of armed conflict: post-Cold War conflicts, called "anarchic" owing to the plethora of players, were killing more civilians than combatants. UNICEF was particularly active in their condemnation, and many NGOs repeated that depressing observation, which was often summed up in two numbers: during World War I, 90% of the victims were soldiers, but from then on the proportions were reversed, with 90% of the victims being nowadays civilians.

Never mind the fact that, in reality, the biggest victims of current conflicts—at least in terms of numbers—are young men of fighting age, and that the 90:10 ratio is more of a talking point than a quantitative estimate. Never mind, also, how hard it is to distinguish civilians from combatants in domestic conflicts, where people can often be both, depending on the moment. What shocks me about that assertion is how it presents the 1914–18 War in a favourable light, in a kind of acceptance of the death of some nine million young men. Because those millions of corpses were wearing a uniform, the "Great War" is the war humanitarians prefer, to paraphrase Georges Brassens. Taking that a bit further, the fifty million men that donned uniforms over those four years were legitimate targets. I see that as *post facto* justification for the pacifists' distrust of anything that might render war acceptable. That that slaughter can be used as an example of respect for humanitarian law without being rejected out of hand is astounding.

Is saying that we're living in a time when there are more and more wars on the planet also debatable?

It's hard to say if the number of wars is changing, whether there are more of them now than during the Cold War, because counting them is complicated. For example, should we include violence from Central American drug cartels, narrowly circumscribed insurrections or military repression? As far as I know, there is no definition of war that would allow a confident response to that question. I'm thinking, for example, of organized crime in Mexico, which has been rising steadily since the 1990s, and which up to 2011 caused more deaths than the war in Afghanistan, at which point the death rate in Mexico seems to have fallen. And the relative mortality, which is measured as a proportion of the total population, is far higher in Honduras and El Salvador than in

Mexico, also due to the drug trade. While these situations are not what we would ordinarily call "war", the mortality levels approach those in armed conflicts.

That's why researchers attempt to assess the number of victims of violence in different situations, as well as mortality trends, but, there again, there are serious methodological problems with defining cases and estimating the number of cases, which explain the large variations among the results. Some studies show that mortality has declined steadily since World War II, and even more since the end of the Cold War, while others question those conclusions based on the inaccuracy of such measurements.

For example, it is agreed, quite rightly, that in addition to direct mortality—deaths caused by projectiles and fragments—we should count indirect mortality—the additional deaths attributable to damage to social structures and the economy. While it does improve our understanding of the impact of armed violence on a society, excess mortality is very hard to evaluate. How much of the excess mortality in Somalia in 1991–2, for example, can be attributed to the war, the drought and government negligence, respectively? Or how much credence should we give the mortality surveys that make the Congo War (1996–2004) the "worst humanitarian crisis since the Second World War", with close to six million dead? That question comes up here not just because there were questionable extrapolations (always a very tricky issue in these mortality surveys), but also because the estimated indirect excess mortality in this case accounted for more than 99% of the total excess mortality. The authors estimated that, overall, for each single death by bullet there were almost a hundred deaths from other causes (most notably malaria and malnutrition) which would not have occurred, or would have been treated, had it not been for the war.

The estimated indirect excess mortality in Darfur from 2004 to 2008 was 2:1; though this seems far more reasonable intuitively, it also leaves room for questions regarding when and where the excess mortality occurred. The epidemiology of disasters, of which the measurement of violence is a component, is an important but inexact science, especially since mortality figures are very often political issues, even for past conflicts. Vietnam, for example, estimates that the war for liberation killed more than three million people, while the United States puts the number at fewer than one million. And, just for the record, I will recall the argument over the mortality figures for the twentieth century's two totalitarian regimes, including the "hundred million deaths" caused by Communism, which would make it even more barbarous than Nazism.

In any case, even assuming that the number of deaths due to armed conflict is declining steadily over the long term, the violence of certain conflicts is evident well beyond the countries where they play out. Media coverage does, of course, play a role in this, but so—especially—does terrorism, whose very strategy is to demoralize people and which has taken on a whole new dimension since the 11 September 2001 attacks. The state of emergency has become part of statutory law in France, with little opposition; there are armed patrols in our streets, fewer people are travelling to countries that had been safe until recently, and so forth. Wars, epidemics and attacks are our daily routine, anxiety-producing and news-making, and many of the conflicts are taking place in Europe's immediate periphery, from Ukraine to Mali, including Syria, Afghanistan and Libya. Ultimately, this perception—objective or not, it doesn't matter—has become a political fact. How the number of war victims is changing tells us nothing about the widely held feeling that we're living in a world more dangerous than it was twenty years ago.

But how is humanitarian law viewed today, as conflicts become more high tech?

The ICRC is the organization responsible for ensuring its respect, promoting it, and helping it evolve; its legal experts are the reference on the subject, since they are its guardians. When talking about how the Geneva Conventions have evolved, I mentioned how humanitarian law—with its 559 articles and its multiple categories of "protected persons" (wounded, prisoners, civilians under occupation, etc.)—has become more complex. The Geneva Conventions were last supplemented in 1977 by the "additional protocols", which brought irregular combatants under international law at the request of some Third World countries. There have been no significant changes for the past forty years, and on several occasions I've heard international legal experts say that, in the current context, any revisions would be a step backward.

That said, given the proliferation of sophisticated weapons such as cluster bombs that spray radio-transparent (and thus undetectable) fragments and detonate unpredictably (and thus indiscriminately), and the DIME bombs I have talked about, I don't think humanitarian law is a useful instrument for controlling these kinds of technological changes. The practicalities of how war is conducted will in any event be left to the discretion of the world's military powers. And a world in which those powers can no longer do that probably wouldn't need humanitarian law anymore.

Henry Dunant talked about creating "oases of humanity" in the flood of violence that is war. I think we should take him up on that. Humanitarians try, with varied but real success, to create such oases of at least some humanity, whether health care settings or places where food and survival kits are distributed. For those who can take advantage of these, they are invaluable—sometimes lifesaving—and worth defending. But they don't change the horrifying reality of war, which is a wrecking ball. Humanitarians, and the principles they claim to stand for, played only a marginal role in the civil and international wars of the twentieth century.

So are you completely disillusioned with humanitarian action?

No, not at all, because the feeling of usefulness I get from my involvement with MSF is not affected. Let's just say that I practise my humanitarianism without being a believer! That's a quip, of course, but what I mean by that is that I think there's excessive reverence for canon—sorry, humanitarian—law in the humanitarian world. Excessive in the sense that believing so strongly in its virtues can cloud our view of the power relationships at work in the real world, and that includes how the law is used. In 2009, for example, during Operation Defensive Shield in Gaza, an Israeli Army lawyer said: "The people who go into a house despite a warning do not have to be taken into account in terms of injury to civilians … From the legal point of view, I do not have to show consideration for them."[6] An American officer said something analogous when announcing a "clean-up" operation to a journalist in Mogadishu in 1993, during Operation Restore Hope.

For political forces in war, whether state or non-state actors, the threshold of what is tolerable depends on their interests. "War crime", for example, refers to excessive cruelty "not justified by military necessity". But who, ultimately, defines what is a "necessity"? The victor, of course. More generally, how the power treats the population will depend on how concerned (or not) it is about earning its goodwill. And it will moderate its brutality according to the importance it attaches to its international image. The US Army has developed software that its targeting officers can use to predict—based on a wide variety of parameters (population density, time of day, type of buildings, and so on)—the collateral damage from bombing urban areas. The objective: to avoid causing more than 29 civilian deaths, because according to its advisers, 30 is the threshold beyond which negative reports appear in the press. That kind of fine detail demonstrates the remarkable pragmatism of an imperial republic. In any case, humanitarian law is by its very nature subject to the logic of war, which is why NGOs should not try to champion it, as is often the case.

So the question for you is not necessarily about rethinking humanitarian law?

Humanitarian law has not "civilized" war—to believe that would require a strong dose of idealism or self-deception—and I don't think we should expect anything of that order. If indiscriminate bombing has (nearly) stopped, it's not because the law forbids it, but because it elicits strong condemnation and thus has a high political cost—and, as I said, because other more "economical" military methods are available. Therefore, in my opinion we should be looking to political mobilization against wars, rather than to the law.

Are we to understand that humanitarian law is useless and that we should simply get rid of it?

No, because humanitarian law helps create a space for negotiating with governments—those that accept the opportunity, naturally, which not all do—I'm thinking of Syria, in particular. But many agree to it. Humanitarian organizations can use humanitarian law to support their requests for permission to act, and to reinforce their status as legitimate actors in conflicts, based on the commitments those governments made. Neither a flag to be waved nor a relic to be dismissed, humanitarian law helps humanitarian organizations find their place in war. That's not nothing, and for that it should be defended. To expect more from it is to forget what it is, deep down, and delude ourselves about its virtues.

I'll give one last example to finish. In October 2016, the ICRC held a round table in Geneva on "Translating humanitarian law into military tactics". The aim was to think about ways to conduct military operations within the limits of humanitarian law, and in particular to consider appropriate, effective and yet legally acceptable rules of armed engagement. The four panellists included two armed forces legal advisers (from NATO and the United States) and a colonel.

This may seem extremely cynical, but that call to incorporate humanitarian law into military tactics is a useful reminder of its origins and approach, which are too often hidden beneath the popular image of the rescuer bent over the victim. And we should also remember what its guardian, the ICRC, is: the sponsor of a diplomatic treaty whose primary interlocutors and ultimate implementers are states. Here, laid bare, is the ambition to civilize warfare—for some, a belief; for others, a technique of make-believe. Everyone knows which they are.

We've learned, from this conversation, that "just" wars are justified after the fact by some highly questionable humanitarian arguments. Is the informed citizen completely powerless in this situation?

I obviously don't believe that wisdom consists of staying out of world affairs and contemplating the world from the outside, like an entomologist, or that humanitarian solidarity is enough to fulfil our duty to humanity. I hope I have sufficiently demonstrated that in our exchange. Nor should military expeditions be condemned on the basis of general principles (like sovereignty or anti-imperialism) while ignoring appalling human realities, but rather on the situations they create.

Guy Hermet, who has studied the democratic transitions in Spain and Latin America, suggests that we define democracy, at a minimum, as the demilitarization of the struggle for power. Though that definition certainly doesn't exhaust the issue, it's a good start, with Libya embodying the negative version. There, power (not just gaining it, but keeping it, because separating the two isn't easy) came from the barrel of a gun. And there it has stayed, under the auspices of a war to protect the rule of law. I'd like to emphasize, now that our conversation is coming to an end, that this contradiction in terms goes hand in hand with using empty language bearing no relation to reality. Yesterday's interlocutor becomes today's enemy of mankind, blackmail is presented as negotiation, an alleged massacre becomes a genocide in progress, and a worn-out lie a defence of humanity's values. Both Arendt and Orwell saw this betrayal of reality by language—said another way, this obliteration of the distinction between fact and fiction—as an essential element of totalitarian power. "The ideal subject of totalitarian rule is not the convinced Nazi or the convinced Communist, but people for whom the distinction between fact and fiction (i.e. the reality of experience) and the distinction between true and false (i.e. the standards of thought) no longer exists."[7]

I am obviously not suggesting that we conflate a plan for total domination—which is what these authors were talking about—with democracy, which would only further such confusion while seeming to condemn it. But we can avoid that regrettable temptation by remembering that the language of even the most defensible grand "causes"—human rights, protecting the most vulnerable—lends itself admirably to all kinds of disguises; the lie becomes a possible step toward the truth, and war a plausible condition of peace. As political scientist Georges Burdeau wrote, "Once we accept the power of magic seven-league boots, everything follows in perfectly logical fashion—both the ogre's shortness of breath and Little Thumb's speed."[8] That sentence could well have been the motto for every one of the situations we've been looking at.

There are undoubtedly justifiable wars, but the justifications must be explained, and that's exactly where the "just war" criteria can help us, as I've tried to show. But there are no "just wars", there are only false prophets. And I worry about how easily their stories, rewritten for the purpose at hand, become History.

NOTES

1. WHAT DO WE MEAN BY "JUST WARS"?

1. André Guichaoua, *From War to Genocide: Criminal Politics in Rwanda, 1990–1994*, translated by Don E. Webster. Madison, University of Wisconsin Press, 2017.

2. Michael Walzer, *Just and Unjust Wars: A Moral Argument with Historical Illustrations*. New York, Basic Books, 2015, p. 122.

3. http://laregledujeu.org/tele-rdj/qui-a-peur-du-devoir-ding-erence/.

4. Walzer, *Just and Unjust Wars*, p. 122.

5. Christian Mellon, "Guerre juste", in *Dictionnaire de la violence*, ed. Michela Marzano. Paris, PUF, 2011. English quotation taken from St Augustine, *The City of God*, Book XIX, Chapter 7, translated by Marcus Dods, http://www.logoslibrary.org/augustine/city/1907.html.

6. The Paris Institute of Political Studies.

7. The FSA is an association of pro-democracy rebel groups. Created in July 2011, it was the main opposition to the government army before being swallowed up by Salafist and Jihadist groups.

2. USING "ALTERNATIVE FACTS" TO JUSTIFY WAR: THE CASE OF LIBYA

1. Respectively Minister of Foreign Affairs and Secretary of State for Human Rights.

2. Simon Leys, *Les Habits neufs du Président Mao*. Paris, Champ Libre, 1971. (*The Chairman's New Clothes: Mao and the Cultural Revolution*, translated by Pierre Ryckmans. New York, St. Martin's Press, 1977.)

3. As cited by Guy Hermet in *Les Désenchantements de la liberté*. Paris, Fayard, 1993.

4. See Fabrice Weissman and Jean-Hervé Bradol, https://www.msf-crash.org/en/publications/war-and-humanitarianism/appeal-darfur-killings-and-demagogy.

5. Bernard-Henri Lévy, *La Guerre sans l'aimer. Journal d'un écrivain au cœur du printemps libyen*. Paris, Grasset, 2011, p. 19.

6. Hugh Roberts, "Who said Gaddafi had to go?", *London Review of Books*, 17 November 2011.

7. https://www.un.org/press/en/2011/sc10187.doc.htm.

8. Patrick Haimzadeh, *Au cœur de la Libye de Kadhafi*. Paris, JC Lattès, 2011, p. 130.

9. Haimzadeh, *Au cœur de la Libye de Kadhafi*.

10. On the Orient XXI and Mediapart websites, in particular, as well as in *Le Monde Diplomatique*.

11. Fabrice Arfi and Karl Laske, *Avec les compliments du guide. Sarkozy-Kadhafi, l'histoire secrète*. Paris, Fayard, 2017.

12. An American expression known as the "Pottery Barn rule".

3. SOMALIA: THE FIRST HUMANITARIAN WAR

1. See John R. MacArthur, "Remember Nayirah, Witness for Kuwait?", *New York Times*, 6 January 1992.

2. Rony Brauman, *Somalia: A Humanitarian Crime*, https://www.msf-crash.org/en/publications/war-and-humanitarianism/somalia-humanitarian-crime. French version published in 1993 by Editions Arléa.

3. More than 1 death per 10,000 per day.

4. Brauman, *Somalia: A Humanitarian Crime*.

4. KOSOVO: A MORALLY JUSTIFIED UNJUST WAR?

1. Henry Kissinger, *Daily Telegraph*, 28 June 1999.
2. See Jean-Baptiste Jeanjène Vilmer, *La Responsabilité de protéger*. Paris, PUF, 2015.

5. AFGHANISTAN AND IRAQ: TWO WARS "FOR CIVILIZATION"

1. French TV series portraying and satirizing the work of NGOs in Afghanistan.
2. French website specialized in critically analyzing the media.
3. Tzvetan Todorov, *The Inner Enemies of Democracy*. Cambridge: Polity Press, 2014.
4. Marc Bloch, *Reflections of a Historian on the False News of the War*, translated by James P. Holoka, http://www.miwsr.com/2013-051.aspx.

6. INTERNATIONAL HUMANITARIAN LAW: LEGAL PIPE DREAM AND THE LANGUAGE OF POWER

1. Enzo Traverso, Pietro Causarano and Valeria Galimi (eds), "Interpréter la guerre", in *Le XXᵉ siècle des guerres*. Paris, Ed. de l'Atelier, 2004, p. 488.
2. Gustave Moynier, *Les Causes du succès de la Croix-Rouge*. Paris, Académie des sciences morales et politiques, 1888.
3. Grégoire Chamayou, *A Theory of the Drone*, translated by Janet Lloyd. New York, The New Press, 2015.
4. See, for example, Jean-Baptiste Jeangène Vilmer, https://www.cairn.info/revue-politique-etrangere-2013–3-page-119.htm.
5. http://readersupportednews.org/news-section2/323–95/17464-from-boston-to-pakistan-pentagon-claims-entire-world-is-a-battlefield.
6. https://www.haaretz.com/1.5069101.

7. Hannah Arendt, *The Origins of Totalitarianism*. New York, Penguin Random House, 2004, Part 3, Ch. 13, § 3.
8. Georges Burdeau, *La Politique au pays des merveilles*. Paris, PUF, 1979.